THE PROSPERITY

TRACK

Energize, Enable, Empower

JAMES R. PETERS, CFA, CFP®

First Priority Publishing
Las Vegas, NV

The Prosperity Track - Energize, Enable, Empower

By James R. Peters, CFA, CFP®

First Priority Publishing
Las Vegas, Nevada
www.firstprioritypublishing.com

The information presented herein represents the views of the author as of the
date of publication. This book is presented for informational purposes only. Due
to the rate at which conditions change, the author reserves the right to alter and
update his opinions at any time. While every attempt has been made to verify the
information in this book, the author does not assume any responsibility for
errors, inaccuracies, or omissions.

Copyediting by Dr. Cheryl Mayfield
Proofreading by Gina Peters, Jim & Marlene Peters, Lisa Buck, and Peter Simon
Cover design by Zizi Iryaspraha S. @ www.pagatana.com

ISBN 978-0989834506
Version 1.1

This book is dedicated to my amazing wife Gina, for without whom, this book would have never been written. Thank you for always believing in me and pushing me to do my very best.

I would like to give special thanks to the many family members, friends, clients, and co-workers who have taught me the true meaning of prosperity. It is with the highest appreciation and gratitude that I pass along your experiences and teachings for others to benefit.

About the Author

James R. Peters leads Integress Financial, where he oversees portfolio management, client financial advisory, and business strategy. With over ten years of experience managing investment portfolios and providing customized financial advice, he has personally assisted hundreds of people along their Prosperity Track.

Prior to co-founding Integress, James was a Senior Investment Associate at The Private Banking and Investment Group of Merrill Lynch & Co., where he was responsible for portfolio management, financial planning, and client communication.

He earned his BS from the University of Nevada, Las Vegas, majoring in both financial services and managerial finance. James holds Chartered Financial Analyst (CFA) and Certified Financial Planner (CFP®) designations.

He is an Illinois native and a die-hard Chicago Bears Fan. James currently resides in Henderson, Nevada with his wife Gina.

Email: james@prosperitytrack.com
Twitter: @ProsperityTrack
Facebook: www.facebook.com/ProsperityTrack
Website: www.prosperitytrack.com

Contents

Introduction

> *A man is not rightly conditioned until he is a happy, healthy, and prosperous being; and happiness, health, and prosperity are the result of a harmonious adjustment of the inner with the outer of the man with his surroundings.*
>
> **James Allen**

What does prosperity mean to you?

Does it mean living in a massive hillside mansion? Traveling to distant lands? Being a respected member of the community? Becoming debt free? Celebrating your one-hundredth birthday at home, surrounded by loving family members? Having a big bank account? The freedom to take long hikes in the woods without looking at your watch? Working because you want to, rather than working because you have to?

Each of us has our own definition of prosperity. *The Prosperity Track* entails developing a vision of prosperity and formulating a plan to achieve it.

Prosperity is not quite the same thing as wealth. While your vision of prosperity may include wealth and valuable possessions, for most people wealth is merely a means to an end. The goal is to enjoy increased personal freedom and self-assurance. This is the essence of true prosperity, which encompasses far more than material items and includes those things money can't buy—things like peace of mind, fulfillment, and a sense of security.

Prosperity isn't a number, it's a feeling. In order to feel prosperous, you need to feel empowered to live a life free of worry.

But prosperity is elusive.

Life is full of challenges. The economy goes up and down. Careers change. Illness and natural disasters strike. And we have our own internal blocks that can hold us back without us recognizing them.

The Prosperity Track is designed to help you gain control of your financial life, so you can focus on the things that bring you joy. Although many people believe prosperity is either dictated by others or is under the control of an unfeeling universe, prosperity can be achieved by everyone. Prosperous individuals live in an enlightened state, and feel prepared to handle all challenges that come their way.

This book contains case studies, tools, examples, and exercises to get you moving in the right direction and to keep you on track. Each of the eight chapters ends with takeaways, thought provoking questions (Prosperity in Practice), and sometimes exercises (Prosperity in Action) to help you reach your full potential.

I have included many examples of people who have overcome great obstacles and achieved a prosperous life. Some examples are celebrities, while others are regular folks who simply wanted a better life. In some cases, the identities and details have been changed to protect the innocent (and the not-so-innocent). Although some names may be fake, the lessons are anything but.

In this book, I'll demonstrate that prosperous does not mean wealthy, just as wealthy does not mean prosperous. Those who are constantly seeking wealth as their ultimate goal, rarely reach a level of contentment. They are never satisfied and continually desire greater financial enrichment. One must look deep inside to find what is driving this need for greater material wealth. You should strive not only to be rich, but to be happy. Understanding what makes you happy is crucial to achieving a life of prosperity. Happiness is an individual feeling and cannot be determined by someone else. Your level of personal satisfaction must come from within.

Staying on the road of prosperity is not a matter of luck and timing; it's a matter of focus and action. *The Prosperity Track* will give you the practical, down to earth tools you need to define prosperity for yourself, analyze your current position, plan your strategy, and put your *Prosperity Plan* into action.

Each of us has the ability to envision and build an amazing lifestyle full of accomplishment and wellbeing. This does not happen by accident or luck, but through dedication and focus. We can unlock our potential for prosperity by managing and overcoming our greatest fears. Success is never easy; just ask anyone who has managed to *become* successful and *stay* successful. But each of us has a unique personality and set of skills. *The Prosperity Track* can help you develop these traits and skills, ultimately achieving a greater life for you and your family or community.

True success should not be viewed as a matter of social status; it's your own definition of success that matters. Your goals and aspirations must be your own and not be influenced by outsiders. If you let others choose for you, you will lack motivation to succeed. Staying on the Prosperity Track means you have what you need and you are comfortable with what you have achieved.

For more than a decade, I have provided financial planning and investment advice to hundreds of people. Through helping others, I was able to learn from people with circumstances different than my own. I learned about prosperity from teachers, police officers, doctors, lawyers, entertainers, professional athletes, business owners, entrepreneurs, retirees, etc. Through these interactions, I realized happiness in life has less to do with money and more to do with attitude.

I am blessed to have worked with such amazing people, who opened my eyes to a world beyond material wealth. Regardless of your current status, ethnicity, gender, age, or income level, I believe you have the ability to achieve your own state of prosperity. Achieving prosperity is not always easy, but I can promise you it is always worth it. I hope *The Prosperity Track* will be your guide on the road of prosperity and to a better life.

Chapter One:

Defining Prosperity

There is no way to prosperity, prosperity is the way.

Wayne Dyer

Let's begin our Prosperity Track journey by talking about what it means to be prosperous. Once we have agreed on a definition, you can decide for yourself whether prosperity is something you should personally strive for. If you agree that it is, then you'll want to keep reading as I reveal the secrets for attaining prosperity.

To begin our exploration, we ask: What does it mean to be prosperous? Where can we look for a consensus as to what defines prosperity?

It's important to understand that prosperity means something different to each one of us. According to *Wikipedia*, prosperity is "the state of flourishing, thriving, good fortune and/or successful social status." The *Merriam-Webster Dictionary* says that it's "the condition of being successful or thriving; especially economic well-being." The *Macmillan Dictionary* puts it quite bluntly: Prosperity is "the situation of being successful and having a lot of money."

Is this true? Let's look at some examples of prosperity.

Consider the person who lives with untold riches that he or she has inherited or has been given. They are rich by birth, or perhaps they've been catapulted into wealth by winning the lottery. He or she knows not how to earn their own money, especially not in the amounts that fill their bank account. If their wealth were to vanish tomorrow, this person would be like a lost lamb in the forest. While their life is filled with luxury cars, fine houses, and maybe even the attention of the paparazzi, is such a person truly prosperous?

How about the ruthless boss who cares only about increasing profits? He or she gives no regard to the people who get hurt in the process. As they tally up the bank deposits, they say to themselves, "The end justifies the means." Skirting the law is no problem because they believe everyone does it, so don't be a sucker and get taken advantage of. It's a dog-eat-dog world and the biggest baddest dog is the one who comes out on top. For this person, material riches are the only gauge of success and should be flaunted for all to see.

Is this person prosperous?

Consider the person who has little money and few comforts, but is nonetheless happy. Such people exist, and they live very simple lives without the desire for expensive cars or big houses. They find other ways to enjoy life, perhaps with their grandchildren, by volunteering, or traveling around the world with only a backpack and a guidebook. They consider wealth burdensome and are unimpressed with material displays of wealth. They've witnessed how others experience anxiety about losing their wealth and they think, "Of all the things I have to lose, wealth is not the one I worry about!"

Could such a person be considered prosperous?

Finally, there's the person who has worked hard and saved their money. They've been successful in business, sports, or the arts. This man or woman enjoys a life of material comfort and has enough wealth to carry them for the foreseeable future. They don't live paycheck to paycheck and can afford to take relaxing vacations to recharge.

Is such a person prosperous?

Then there's the person who is striving for a goal but hasn't yet reached it. This person is the actor who is still playing bit parts and looking for their big break. They're dreaming of a bright future and the dream sustains them. Perhaps they feel they're the next Thomas Edison—they're trying to solve a difficult problem, and while they may fail over and over again they never give up.

Could they be considered prosperous?

What Prosperity Looks Like

For the purposes of this book, we'll define prosperity as:

The personal state of achievement, contentment, and wellbeing.

Achievement, contentment, and wellbeing are all subjective attributes. Note that measurable monetary wealth is not part of my definition. While wealth is an aspect of wellbeing, it's not the most important measure of prosperity. Most human beings wouldn't feel prosperous if they couldn't pay for life's necessities. Prosperity is achieved by accumulating enough wealth to satisfy your needs and maintain the lifestyle *you choose*. Once a maintenance level of wealth has been achieved, additional wealth does not necessarily result in a higher level of prosperity or happiness. In its simplest term, prosperity is having a steady supply of what you need when you need it. Because everyone has a different lifestyle, it's important to determine your ideal prosperous lifestyle.

People often confuse wealth and prosperity. Wealth refers to material things, while prosperity refers to a state of wellbeing. Society may have an opinion of who's wealthy and who isn't, but prosperity is personal by nature and cannot be defined by anyone other than you. To some, a desired state of prosperity may be realized by living each day without having to work. It may involve a glamorous lifestyle of exotic travel and fast cars. For others, their work itself is so enjoyable that no matter how much money they earn, they remain eager to go to the office every day! It's not because they have an insatiable desire to have more money than the next person; it's because they simply enjoy what they do. They find work more pleasurable than sitting at home watching TV and eating chips.

Prosperous people are not always easy to identify. They don't always live in mansions or drive expensive cars. They have enough wealth to support themselves comfortably. It does not necessarily mean they cannot afford to buy these things, it means they are happy enough without them. The opposite is also true. Those who buy expensive cars, homes, and jewelry are not necessarily prosperous. Many people purchase these items to display an image of wealth and prosperity, when in reality they have neither.

Wealth is relative and based on social norms. On a small tropical island where people have few material possessions, a man without a goat may be considered very poor while a man with five goats may be considered very wealthy. In a place where there are vast livestock farms and ranches, that same man who owns nothing but his five goats would be considered very poor indeed. Unless you happen to be Bill Gates—who as of this writing is the richest person on the planet with estimated wealth of $72.7 billion —there's always someone richer. And, unless you own the 590 foot Azzam, the world's largest private yacht, someone always has a bigger boat.

It's not always easy to tell who has wealth. Many wealthy people "dress down" and drive ordinary cars. They have their own set of interests and may not want to display their wealth for the world to see. Surprisingly, some wealthy individuals actually consider the management of their wealth a burden. This is a problem many people would love to have.

In December 2012, officials in Carson City, Nevada announced that a substitute teacher from California was the sole heir to a fortune of gold coins found in the home of her reclusive cousin who had died the previous June. Genealogical researchers hired to find the relatives of Walter Samaszko, Jr. determined that Arlene Magdon was the sole living heir to what appraisers said was an estate worth more than $7.4 million. After Samaszko died at his modest ranch-style home, a cleaning crew entered the property and found enough gold coins and bullion to fill two wheelbarrows. The sixty-nine-year-old Samaszko had lived in Nevada's capital city since the late 1960s. He was a modest man, and if you saw him on the street you'd never suspect he was wealthy. Records show he withdrew only about $500 a month to pay household bills. He died with $1,200 in a personal checking account and slightly more than $165,000 in a money market and mutual fund account.

Samaszko kept meticulous records of the family's coin purchases dating back to at least 1964, when gold averaged about $35 per ounce. At the time of his death, gold sold for nearly $1,600 an ounce. Authorities believe Samaszko's mother, who lived with him until her death in 1992, had purchased most of the coins.

Walter Samaszko was certainly wealthy, and appeared to have his expenses under control. By every measurement he could have been very prosperous, but was he? This we will never know. We can conclude with some certainty, however, that he took great pleasure in *amassing* his fortune, but took no pleasure in *spending* it.

Other people go to great lengths to appear wealthy while struggling to keep up with their financial obligations. I need not cite any examples of such people; you probably know more than one of them in your own family, at work, or in your social circle.

Fortunately, financial difficulties can be remedied. With corrective action, no hole is too deep to climb out from.

What Prosperity Feels Like

It's difficult to look at someone and determine whether they're prosperous or not. Certainly, if you see a homeless person begging on the street, it's a good bet he or she would not think of themselves as prosperous. Prosperous individuals feel they have what they need and can be considered worry free. Such a feeling can only come from preparation and understanding.

There's a big difference between "worry free" and "carefree." Worry free is achieved through planning, dedication, hard work, and discipline. It's the knowledge that you have a sustainable level of wealth and income to do the things you want to do.

Because they have very few responsibilities and demands, children act carefree. They eat when they're hungry and fall asleep when they're tired. When they see a toy they like, they want it *now*. Adults who act in a carefree manner are concerned with immediate gratification, rather than long-term prosperity. Truly carefree adults impulsively think about life only in the present context and have no eye towards the future. They may act in a way that is oblivious to the world around them, unaware of the impact of their actions.

Living a carefree life rarely leads to prosperity, and a prosperous life is rarely carefree. The fact is people who are carefree on the outside may be more stressed than they want you to believe. They may feel powerless in controlling their lives, and accept whatever comes along with a shrug. They say, "What can you do?" as disaster strikes. Such people, as kind-natured as they may be, feel like victims whose lives are solely in the hands of fate. They believe their decisions really don't matter.

Worry free living is rarely accidental and is often many years in the making. As we grow older, we face difficult decisions that have the potential to profoundly influence our lives. Decisions surrounding finances and health have long lasting effects. The longer the time period during which poor decisions are made, the harder it is to change. Those leading a prosperous life have figured out what they need, and have a system for getting it. This gives them an inner serenity that's obvious to anyone who meets them.

Hoping and wishing are not a plan for prosperity. When it comes to your long-term health and happiness, nothing should be left to chance.

What Prosperity Isn't

Prosperity is achieved through preparation, dedication, and discipline, not by luck or chance. Many people think wealth alone will make them feel prosperous. Unfortunately, this is not the case. Wealth may solve your immediate needs, but it rarely lasts without discipline. Too many times, we hear about athletes and performers who amass fortunes, only to see them penniless a few short years later.

Although wealth may help, the satisfaction of deeper needs makes us prosperous. Have you ever heard the saying, "money can't buy happiness?" Most of us believe we would be happier if we had more money. But money alone does not guarantee happiness. Have you ever met someone who was wealthy, but constantly miserable? If so, you may have thought, "this person is rich, why are they so unhappy?" It's what you do with your money that makes you prosperous.

Money can be a powerful tool for good. Wealth, when achieved through legal and ethical means, can have a positive impact on the lives of many. The charitable efforts of Bill Gates and Warren Buffett, the two richest people in America, are nothing less than astounding. Through inspiration and influence, the Gates' and Buffett have convinced more than a hundred of the world's wealthiest people to give away the majority of their wealth to charity. Their commitments are viewable at www.givingpledge.org.

Prosperity isn't accidental. Years of responsible living can mean the difference between prosperity and poverty. You are only entitled to the air you breathe; everything else in this world must be paid for. A large bank account alone does not determine your level of happiness, although it may determine your level of satisfaction. Money is needed to buy life's essentials. Without having your own supply, you must rely on others to support your lifestyle. To some, being supported by someone else is more painful than earning it themselves.

Prosperity isn't easy. It's much easier to live each day as it comes, with no concern for the future. Planning and saving takes discipline and sacrifice. A long-term focus is mandatory for those choosing to be prosperous. It takes discipline and faith to trade immediate gratification for greater rewards later.

For example, consider the person who wins millions of dollars in the lottery. Suddenly they face a profound choice: they can buy whatever material goods they want, or they can learn to be responsible stewards of their new wealth and enjoy a life of stability and, yes, prosperity. The National Endowment for Financial Education estimates that as many as seventy percent of people who land sudden windfalls lose that money within several years. Most of them spend their wealth on houses, cars, and vacations, or give it away to friends and family. They go from an ordinary existence to vast wealth, and then bankruptcy.

David Gehle is a positive example. In 2006, after spending twenty years working at a ConAgra Foods meatpacking plant in Nebraska, he and seven co-workers won a $365 million Powerball jackpot. He left ConAgra three weeks after winning and used some of his prize to travel the world. But he invested most of his winnings, and eventually bought a $450,000 home in a tidy neighborhood on the southern edge of his native town of Lincoln, Nebraska. The day he got his winning check from the lottery commission, David Gehle was wealthy, not prosperous. He had a long road ahead of him with many potential pitfalls. And after seven years of sensibly managing his fortune, you might say that David Gehle is now a prosperous man.

Who Is Prosperous?

Prosperous people are those who have achieved their ideal lifestyle through visualization, planning, and execution. They lead a fulfilled life free of worries. By defining their ideal lifestyle, they were able to plan and work towards that distinct goal. As a reminder, prosperity is a state of mind that can only be defined by oneself. No one can dictate what another's ideal prosperous lifestyle looks like.

For a few people, sudden wealth brings the potential for either disaster or long-term prosperity. David Gehle, the lottery winner, is one of those rare people whose inner fortitude enabled them to transition from wealthy to prosperous. In the news and on TV, we see countless examples of people who obtain significant wealth suddenly. Many of them bask in the glory of their new wealth, only to fade into obscurity as they fail to achieve a state of prosperity. The most recent examples of this are reality TV stars who are vaulted from obscurity to great wealth, and lack the inner strength to manage their windfall. People often think life would be "perfect" if only they were rich. But prosperity, as opposed to wealth, is a state of mind complementing financial security. Prosperity is achieved and earned, but never granted.

Anyone can be prosperous. The man who lives on a small tropical island and who owns five goats may live his entire life in blissful prosperity. He has everything he wants, and sees no need to acquire more wealth.

Consider the residents of the island of Okinawa. Called "the land of the immortals" in ancient Chinese legends, Okinawa is renowned for the longevity of its residents. For each 100,000 inhabitants there are an average of thirty-five who are aged one hundred or older, which is the highest rate in the world. Inhabitants of Okinawa reach average ages of eighty-six for women and seventy-eight for men.

Are they truly prosperous, or are they simply living longer in a decrepit condition? It's remarkable that Okinawans reach advanced ages, but it's even more impressive when you consider the manner in which they age. Research shows that Okinawans have lower risk of heart attack, stroke, cancer, osteoporosis, and Alzheimer's. They don't just live longer they live better.

On the streets of Okinawa, you may see a ninety-year-old riding a motorbike. They typically walk several kilometers daily, practice karate, kendo, dance, and work in their vegetable gardens. There are no fitness centers or gyms on Okinawa; they practice tai chi and do gardening or other outdoor activities that help reduce their stress level. Many Okinawans belong to close-knit social networks that make them feel connected to their fellow citizens and their environment. Elderly people on Okinawa have surprisingly low depression levels. But they don't have great wealth or own a lot of stuff. In fact, the Okinawa Prefecture is the poorest province of Japan.

Are they prosperous?

It's not always easy to tell who is prosperous and who isn't. For more than a half-century Herbert and Dorothy Vogel worked as civil servants in New York City while assembling what many experts call one of the most important post-1960s art collections in the United

States. In their rent-controlled one-bedroom apartment on Manhattan's Upper East Side, they amassed over 4,782 works of modern art. They displayed their art within their home and had so many remaining pieces, they were forced to store them in closets and under the bed. The couple used only Dorothy's income to cover their living expenses. Instead of eating in expensive restaurants or travelling to exotic places, they used Herb's income, which was never more than $23,000 annually, to buy art. In 1992, the Vogels felt their art should be accessible by the public and decided to transfer the entire collection to the National Gallery of Art. Today, the Vogel collection is estimated to be worth hundreds of millions of dollars.

If you had passed Herb and Dorothy Vogel on the street in Manhattan, you would never have characterized them as prosperous, especially by the standards of the Upper East Side. Their bank account was never very large, because they typically spent extra money on art. They lived well, but not excessively. Their prudent lifestyle enabled them to pursue their passion and accumulate an amazing collection of artwork. They knew exactly what they wanted to do and they planned accordingly. They were playing the game of life for the long run. The Vogels recognized that life was not a sprint but a marathon. Could there have been a happier or more secure couple anywhere?

Income, a potential builder of wealth, is distributed unevenly across the United States. Although rich and poor people live in every state, the average per capita personal income varies tremendously. The United States' median income is $42,693. In Washington, D.C., the 2012 per capita personal income was a hefty $74,710. Yet, Washington D.C. has some of the worst slums in America. The highest income states are Connecticut ($58,908), Massachusetts ($54,687), and New Jersey ($53,628). Which states have the lowest income? Mississippi ($33,073), Idaho ($33,749), and South Carolina ($34,266).

But we now know that Okinawa, which is a relatively poor island, has residents who live long and happy lives. Does income matter? That's hard to tell. But here's some additional statistics: the top five US states for longevity are Hawaii, Minnesota, California, New York, and Connecticut. The top two—Hawaii and Minnesota—lie in the middle of the income chart, with median incomes of $44,024 and $46,227 respectively. In terms of life expectancy, the bottom five US states are Mississippi, West Virginia, Alabama, Louisiana, and Oklahoma, which are at the lower end of personal income. Mississippi is hit twice: it has both the lowest income and the shortest life expectancy of any state in the union. Although higher income may be unrelated to higher life expectancy, low income may in fact be related to shortened life expectancy. Having enough money to provide life's essentials is a crucial aspect of prosperity. Without your physiological needs (food, water, shelter, clothing, etc.) being met, it is impossible to achieve a sense of contentment and wellbeing.

Since anyone can be prosperous, does it matter what profession you choose? The top paying profession in the United States is neurosurgeon, with a median pay of $368,000 a year. Other top-paying professions include petroleum engineer, nurse anesthetist, dentist, actuary, software architect, and pharmacist. Like neurosurgeons, these professions require significant education and dedication. Due to the high level of income, choosing one of these professions could increase the odds of becoming prosperous, but it is not guaranteed. Finding fulfillment in your work is even more important than income. Careers with the highest level of satisfaction include clergy, firefighters, physical therapists, authors, teachers, and artists. Although no job is perfect, make sure you choose an occupation that complements your vision of prosperity.

Nevertheless, just because you get a big paycheck doesn't mean you know how to manage your money. Prosperity can easily vanish with an ugly divorce, gambling, bad investments, a real estate collapse, or just bad planning. Landing a high-paying job only opens the door to prosperity; it does not guarantee it.

Take musicians for instance. Over the past fifty years, we've seen enough rock and pop music stars come and go to understand what it takes to turn financial success into true prosperity. According to most sources, the richest rocker is Bono, the lead singer of U2, who is reportedly worth a cool one billion dollars. We know Bono is rich, but is he prosperous? He is an acclaimed musician, a thriving business man, and continues to demonstrate his commitment to making the world a better place. Bono is an activist for many causes and supports many organizations that do not have a strong global voice. Although praised and criticized for his activism, he pursues his passions and continues to "rock out." He has chosen to live his life based on his personal guiding values.

Here's an interesting fact: among the richest entertainers are Rolling Stones frontman Mick Jagger and his bandmate Keith Richards, who's reportedly worth $276 million. Now Keith Richards has the public image of a guy who barely knows what city he's in, much less having the ability to balance a checkbook. He seems like the kind of person who would squander every penny he has ever earned. Clearly he's better at managing his money than his often disheveled appearance would suggest, or at least he's smart enough to follow the advice of reputable accountants and financial advisors. Is Keith Richards a prosperous man? He's been pursuing his music career for fifty years and he's financially secure. He's in a stable marriage and has a bunch of grown kids who stay out of the tabloids—no scandals there—and his business, the Rolling Stones, is rolling right along. He must be doing something right!

I won't burden you with the other side of the coin—the long list of entertainers and musicians who have earned fortunes only to squander them. Professional athletes, for example, have notoriously short careers and must conserve their wealth in order for it to last. In few instances does a person earn the bulk of his or her wealth in their early twenties and retire in their mid to late twenties. Although rich with income during their playing years, an athlete's ability to earn income from competition is short lived. And unfortunately, too many don't begin planning for life after sports until it's too late. Once the income stops, it's only a matter of time before you see which athletes were smart with their money and which ones were not.

Prosperity shouldn't end when your income stops. Through proper planning and managing your resources, it is possible to continue a prosperous life in retirement. Your choices determine whether you are prosperous today and whether you will be in the future.

How Is Prosperity Achieved?

Prosperity is achieved by reaching deep inside yourself and learning what creates joy and satisfaction within you. By understanding what makes you happy, you can better map out a path that can lead you to a prosperous life. And by understanding how you got where you are today, you can better conquer challenges and overcome your behavioral tendencies. Once you conquer your fears and obstacles, you can be on your way to prosperity.

Let's get down to the nuts and bolts of achieving prosperity. Imagine you could design your life beginning today. This is an activity very few people actually carry out. We get too caught up in the day-to-day pace of life and are unable to step back and take a broad view of our life's direction. We don't see the big picture, and we make decisions based on what seems to be the best option at the moment. If a promotion is offered, we take it without thinking about the long-term effects, focusing only on what we could do with the extra income. We choose our college major based on some idea of its usefulness or the opinions of friends and family. Perhaps we enter a certain profession because our parents want us to. This is what happened to Michael Jackson. He didn't choose to become a singer; his father trained him to be one from an early age. He never knew any other profession or considered any other possibilities.

Take a step back and design your life. How would you achieve prosperity? I'm not talking about get-rich-quick schemes. Winning the lottery is not a plan for prosperity. I'm talking about building a career and a life that will sustain you and your loved ones for decades, giving you financial freedom and a sense of peace and security.

How will you achieve prosperity? One key aspect of success is finding what you love to do, and having the financial means to do it. We repeatedly hear that prosperous people work very hard, and yet they insist what they do doesn't feel like work. Because they enjoy their work, they're willing to do it each and every day with contentment and focus. They get better at what they do simply because they strive for excellence every day. When you are paid to do what you truly love, it's impossible to give a lackluster effort. There are three factors necessary to feeling fulfilled in your career:

1. Do what you love.
2. Do what you are great at.
3. Get paid to be passionate.

When these three factors are present in your career, amazing things seem to happen. You will find your stride and feel empowered to take on challenges you never dreamed of. Employees and business owners who achieve these factors in their work are engaged and ultra-productive. Positive momentum in your career can be instrumental in achieving prosperity.

Sustained effort leads to prosperity, because to prosper you need to provide value to other people. Only after you provide value to others will they in turn reward *you* with value.

One signature trait of prosperous people is that they never stop learning. For them, learning is a lifelong journey. It may take the form of earning one or more college degrees, but it may also take the form of attending adult education classes in the evening or on weekends. The world is full of prosperous people who educated themselves while holding down full time jobs. If you're not in school, you can continue your education by reading books or simply by associating with people who have knowledge to offer. Knowledge can come from a variety of sources; don't be afraid to explore non-traditional methods of learning.

Opportunities for learning are all around us. Unless you enter a profession such as medicine, law, or engineering, your education doesn't have to come from books. Keith Richards, whom I mentioned in the last section as being very prosperous, dropped out of Sidcup Art College to pursue his music career. The only reason he was at Sidcup in the first place was that he had been expelled from Dartford Technical High School. While book learning was clearly not his style, he relentlessly studied music and taught himself how to play blues and rock guitar. What he lacked in formal education, he made up by dedicating himself to his craft and his career. Education can be acquired not only in a classroom but also through sheer drive and determination.

Misconceptions

A discussion of the characteristics of prosperity would not be complete without talking about the misconceptions surrounding prosperity. Knowing what will prevent you from becoming prosperous is just as important as knowing what will get you on the road of prosperity. Here are a few of the common misconceptions about prosperity:

It's a destination. Not really. You'll notice in the previous paragraph I didn't say "road to prosperity" but "road of prosperity." It's true that prosperity is a state of being, but it's also a process. As you progress through the years, your life will undoubtedly change. You'll get older, your job may change, you may move from one city to another, or you may have more or less income. But if you stay on the Prosperity Track, these things will not matter and you'll overcome life's challenges both big and small. Prosperity is about the journey, not just the destination.

It's luck or good timing. Prosperity is reached not through luck but through visualization, planning, and execution. Those who have achieved wealth through luck are the most likely to lose it. As we have seen, this is particularly common with lottery winners and reality show performers.

It's from family or inheritance. Although a great deal of wealth is passed down from generation to generation, this is uncommon. Only a very small number of people inherit enough money to be indefinitely wealthy.

It's not for everyone. On the contrary, anyone can be prosperous. You don't have to be overly intelligent or extremely talented. Anyone with desire and drive can achieve prosperity. Although prosperity may look different from one person to another, the feeling is the same.

It's not for someone with my circumstances. Every one of us can make up excuses as to why we are not able to achieve prosperity. Until you understand what is holding you back, you cannot move forward. Life is about choices. You can either choose to move ahead or not. Just because you haven't made the choice to move ahead doesn't mean that you haven't made any choice. Accepting the lifestyle and circumstances you currently face is a choice.

I'm too far behind. It doesn't matter who you are or where you are in life. Your vision of prosperity must be shaped based on your level of dedication and opportunities. Opportunities are abundant if you choose to look for them. Visualization and focus can lead you to a path you have only dreamed of. To avoid getting further behind, you must act now and be relentless!

I'm too young or too old. It's never too early or late to believe in prosperity. Prosperity is attained by overcoming challenges with creative solutions. You are only limited by your own imagination and hard work. Today is yesterday's tomorrow. Where you are today is a result of what you did yesterday, but tomorrow remains unwritten. Don't let any more time go by without righting the ship.

It must happen overnight. Sorry, there are no quick fixes. Most overnight successes are years in the making. There are no short cuts to prosperity. Wealth achieved quickly and easily is often lost in the same manner. A prosperous life takes effort and time to reach its full potential. Patience and commitment will determine your ultimate fate.

Chapter One Takeaways

As you can see, anyone anywhere can achieve prosperity. The power has always been within you, it is now time to unleash it. You now stand at an important crossroad. You can choose to continue on your current path or try something new. The road ahead will cause you to think and ponder in ways you haven't before, which may be uncomfortable. Prosperity is a process that requires effort and discipline. I urge you to continue along the Prosperity Track and achieve your greatest potential. You deserve it!

Prosperity in Practice

What does prosperity mean to you?

How would prosperity feel to you?

How would you know if you were prosperous?

Who do you know that is prosperous?

Chapter Two

Becoming Prosperous

> *Even if you're on the right track, you'll get run over if you just sit there.*
>
> **Will Rogers**

The first step towards achieving any goal, including prosperity, is to define the goal and fix the image of it in your mind. As I revealed in Chapter One, prosperity is:

The personal state of achievement, contentment, and wellbeing.

You must decide what this means to you. I will give you suggestions and examples, as I did in Chapter One, but ultimately only you can envision your prosperous life. Your personal Prosperity Track may include a house or houses, family, a rewarding career, good health, hobbies, social relationships, a respected place in your community, etc. The visible evidence of prosperity will vary from person to person, but the essence does not. What passes for prosperity in midtown Manhattan may not look like prosperity in the hills of North Dakota. What a young single man wants in a prosperous lifestyle may look different from what his grandmother visualizes. But underneath the exterior trappings, the core values are quite similar.

Once you have envisioned your future prosperity, the next step is to get familiar with the landscape. If you don't know where you're going, how will you know when you get there? In a sense, it's like creating a mental template or a roadmap for prosperity. This is what I'll discuss in Chapter Two. Later, I will help you build your foundation for prosperity by first analyzing your current position. You can't get where you want to go unless you first know where you are! Then we'll create your *Prosperity Plan* and put it into action. I'll share tools that will help you track your progress. There will be no guesswork and no conjecture. From now on, you are going to be in control of your destiny. You'll know how much money you make, how much you spend, and how much you save. You'll know every day how close you are to achieving prosperity. It will feel rewarding because the essence of prosperity is the satisfaction you get from being in control of your life. You'll see that prosperity is not a destination, it's a *process.* And enjoying the process is a big part of living the prosperous life.

What It Takes to Be Prosperous

Now that you have a better understanding of prosperity, the next step is to see whether you're cut out for it. I'm just kidding—I *know* you're cut out for it. You can be prosperous. What I'm going to show you in this chapter is the road of prosperity. The road of prosperity is long and winding, and may have a few hills and even a pothole or two. But there's nothing you can't handle, and I'll remind you that simply staying on the road is ninety percent of prosperity. And hey, you may even discover there are some fun sights along the way.

The power has always been within you, now is the time to unlock your true potential and achieve happiness. Let's explore what it takes to be prosperous.

Personal Habits

Visualization – It's important to take the time to visualize what it means to be prosperous. Unless you have an idea of what you are working towards, you will never get there. By visualizing what it will take to make you feel prosperous—which is what this chapter will help you do—you can formulate a game plan to get you there. When things get difficult, you can close your eyes and remember what you're striving for. These mental pictures can help further identify what you wish to accomplish. You can take it a step further and create a visual representation of your vision. You can create a prosperity board by cutting out pictures depicting your vision of prosperity and attaching them to a poster board. If you are tech savvy, you can also establish a Pinterest® account and collect images and videos online that inspire you. You can view and share images and videos for added inspiration. You can learn more at www.pinterest.com.

Attitude – Your view of prosperity is shaped by your attitude. One person's ideal prosperous lifestyle will be different from another's. While some people wish to be rich and the envy of others, those seeking true prosperity want to feel secure. If you are chasing riches and fame, prosperity is not what you seek. You may be seeking something to compensate for a feeling of insecurity deep inside of you. Those seeking only to impress others will never be prosperous. When your goals ignore your own happiness, you have no control. Prosperity requires control over your own destiny. Your ideal lifestyle can only be defined by you. If you are working only to curry the favor of others, you will lose sight of your own goals. You must focus on what it means for *you* to be happy and lead a fulfilled life.

Behavior – What we do is always more important than what we say. Behavior is what gets things done. We must act in order to be successful. Talk is cheap. Your actions and the choices you make evolve directly from your attitude. Everything you do will either bring you closer to your vision of prosperity or drive you further from it. For example, if you believe your job is drudgery and the only reason you show up is to get a paycheck, then your attitude will manifest itself in your behavior. If you are unhappy in your job, determine what is making you unhappy. Is it something that is unique to that occupation or company? If so, take action and make a change. This is easier said than done, since career changes can have a ripple effect through many other areas of your life. Consider your skills and opportunities and do what is in your best interest. In the interim, try and find something that you enjoy about your work and try not to be distracted by negative aspects. As the saying goes, "fake it 'til you make it."

Have you ever been treated rudely by a clerk in a department store or a waiter in a restaurant? If so, then you have encountered someone whose negative attitude is reflected in their behavior. Unhappy workers never deliver exceptional results. Conversely, if you've ever received exceptional service, you felt the person's positive attitude reflected in their behavior. It's inevitable—you cannot hide your attitude. You owe it to yourself to do something you love, because then your positive attitude will come shining through in every aspect of your life.

Dedication – Prosperity takes time and focus. The Prosperity Track is filled with twists and turns. It's easy to go astray. Although you may get off the track at times, you must have the dedication to get back on. What can help you stay on the track is your plan, and the knowledge that the longer you are able to stay on course, the sooner you will achieve a prosperous life and the longer you will remain prosperous.

Energize – Energy is a major driver of attitude. When you feel lethargic, you will be operating well below your potential. It is important to occasionally take breaks and reenergize. Stress can negatively impact your mental and physical state. Find a positive outlet for pent up stress. Find a place, person, or activity that helps you unwind and relax. Positive energy propels you toward prosperity, while negative energy steers you from it.

Enable – Seek out people and information that can enable you to achieve your vision of prosperity. Positive influences can be very motivational and inspiring. By learning new skills and considering decisions with respect to your ideal lifestyle, you will be enabled to live the life you want to live.

Empowerment – Prosperity is about empowerment. The ability to reach prosperity is within each one of us. We can effect change and improve our lives. Our destiny is in our control. From visualization comes attitude, and from attitude comes behavior, and from behavior comes empowerment. Once you reach a state of empowerment, you can take control of your life and achieve true prosperity. You will be an unstoppable force once you set your mind to it.

Skills

Achieving prosperity takes not only the right attitude and personal habits, but also a set of real-world skills. After all, unless your idea of prosperity is to live in a cave and wear an animal skin, you're going to have to manage your household, relationships, investments, and budget. These things can contribute to a feeling of security, making you feel prosperous indeed.

Budgeting – By understanding and controlling your finances, you'll be able to make better decisions concerning your income and expenses. The biggest pothole in the road of prosperity is lack of control over your own money. This is surprising—after all, it's *your money*. Why wouldn't you keep track of it? It's extremely important to know what you make and precisely where it goes. With today's online banking services, you can track your accounts from a computer, tablet, or smartphone. You don't even have to keep a paper checkbook balance—you can do it all online.

Income – Many people choose only to look to their employer for income. Income opportunities are all around us. We have great flexibility in what we earn, although we don't always realize it. If needed, look for ways to increase your income. Whether we invest or exchange time and expertise for money, we have the ability to adjust or augment our income. Some income streams are permanent while others are temporary; it's up to you to recognize the difference and plan accordingly. Things change that are beyond your control, so be careful not to overextend yourself based on a temporary level of income. An increase to your income, even if only temporary, is still a benefit to be taken advantage of.

Managing expenses – Smart and savvy expense management is vital to reaching prosperity. Whether working or in retirement, expenses must be understood and properly managed. The Prosperity Track system features many valuable tools that will help you manage your expenses and ensure that you're always running your household "in the black" and staying ahead of your obligations. Visit www.prosperitytrack.com/tools for worksheets and tools that will help you along your journey.

Flexibility – There is no single route to prosperity. You must keep an open mind as to what is happening around you. Life will be full of obstacles and opportunities. While it's admirable to have a goal and dedicate yourself to reaching it, it's also necessary to stand ready to make adjustments at any time. It's possible that you could suffer a setback through no fault of your own—the company you work for may be sold and there could be layoffs, or you or a loved one may suffer an unexpected illness. It's also possible you may become inspired to change careers. Whatever the reason, things change and it's important to be adaptable.

Planning – Prosperity does not happen by accident. The goal must be defined and a plan formulated for its achievement. The Prosperity Track system can help you create a plan that's long range, detailed, and practical. You will chart your progress and make adjustments along the way. Remember, while a plan is clear and comprehensive, it's not set in stone. It's designed to serve you, not the other way around!

Case Studies

Let's explore some examples of people who became prosperous and those who didn't.

Consider the case of Maggie. A typical middle-class American student, she attended a four-year college and then went to graduate school. She did well and soon after graduation, she was able to land a job making $45,000 a year.

But Maggie faced a huge challenge: she owed $25,000 in student loan debt. The interest rate was low, but having to pay off massive student loans was worrisome. Maggie wanted to buy a house someday, but with a mountain of debt, it could be impossible.

Maggie decided to take the road less traveled and pay off her student loans as quickly as possible. This meant making a budget for herself and sticking to it, regardless of temptations. Instead of getting her own apartment, she found a roommate and cut her rent expense in half. Instead of buying an expensive car, she opted for a used economy model. She allowed herself to have one credit card, which she used only for emergencies; for everyday purchases, she used her debit card. Her goal was to pay off her loans in two years (twenty-four months), which meant she had to budget a little over a thousand dollars a month for debt repayment. This was roughly one-third of her income, which was a considerable sacrifice. Through practical budgeting and by avoiding opulent purchases, Maggie achieved her goal. Two years after graduation, and living on an average salary, Maggie was debt free and on the road of prosperity. Her next goal? Buy a house in a good neighborhood, which she did a few years later. Many of her peers—the ones who drove fancy cars and shopped at upscale malls—were still heavily burdened by debt, paying only the minimum due on their credit cards and wondering if they would ever live prosperously.

Tony and Teri are also great examples of lifestyle choices. In their twenties, having no prior experience in show business, Tony and Teri were hired to be on a new reality show. Neither had acted before and neither had any experience in managing wealth. To their amazement, and to the amazement of TV critics who thought the show was lousy, the program was a big hit. The stars of the show became overnight celebrities and within three years, each was making two hundred thousand dollars a year. It was more money than either one had ever imagined earning.

The show lasted five years before being cancelled. During that time Tony and Teri each earned enough money to feel wealthy. They did this without any unique skills or achievement, which is rare. In a sense, they had won the lottery. The difference between them and the average lottery winner was that Tony and Teri both became national celebrities.

They both felt rich—but were either Tony or Teri prosperous? Remember that true prosperity is long term. It takes dedication to develop and can last a lifetime. So we need to check in with Tony and Teri a few years after the show ended for an update.

It turns out that Tony seized his opportunity to become prosperous. He took his earnings from the show and invested in a branded "Tony" clothing line and a line of men's cologne. He worked hard to promote his business and was diligent about leading the people working for him. Tony worked with a reputable accounting firm and invested his profits in a diversified portfolio. Five years after the show was cancelled, Tony was a prosperous business owner who owned a thriving clothing and personal products company.

Teri made different choices. She took her paychecks from the show and bought an expensive beachside condo and a luxury car. She took lavish vacations and worked with accountants who encouraged her to invest in offshore tax shelters. Her posse included many hangers-on who spent her money at nightclubs on expensive champagne. Five years after the show was cancelled, Teri was broke. She had to sell her home and car to pay the IRS back taxes. As for her posse, having no more free rides, they quickly abandoned her. Having no skills to make money, Teri had to take parts in low-budget reality shows just to pay the rent on her tiny apartment.

Tony and Teri both had the same opportunity to achieve prosperity. Tony chose to plan for the future, and was able to lead a worry-free life full of challenge and adventure. Teri chose to live a carefree life, and ended up leading a life of borderline poverty, paycheck to paycheck, with no security.

It's Simple, But Not Easy

The Prosperity Track is simple, but not easy. Although many of the concepts and activities in this book may be construed as common sense, I can assure you they are not common practice. Defining your ideal lifestyle and formulating a plan merely takes following a simple set of instructions. However staying on the track is not easy. It's much easier to stray and act irresponsibly.

Take the example of Maggie I cited previously. Her path to prosperity was not complicated. Her plan consisted of one simple goal: put aside a thousand dollars a month to pay off her student loans and get out of debt. In Maggie's case, the simplicity of her plan was a very good thing. Her goal could not have been more straight forward.

But achieving her goal took determination and fortitude. Every day, she experienced temptations that could have pulled her off track, but she remained strong and visualized what she was striving for. Here are a few of the challenges she faced:

The temptation to fritter away her money on little things. It's amazing how many opportunities we face daily to spend money without thinking. Gourmet coffee for five dollars. A Danish for two dollars. A lottery ticket for two dollars. We don't always think about small purchases, but over time, they can drain our bank accounts.

Keeping up with the Joneses. In Maggie's case, it was keeping up with her fashionable girlfriends that was concerning. The compulsion to shop is powerful, especially when you are young and your social circle is fashion conscious. You too want to be stylish and wear the latest fashions. Maggie was a smart shopper who refused to pay the full retail price without a fight, and only bought clothes she knew she would wear often. Every time she passed up the opportunity to spend her money on a trendy fashion, she said to herself, "I'm not going to buy a trend—I'd rather buy my freedom!"

The costs of socializing. It's hard not hanging out with friends after work and on the weekends, running up tabs at local restaurants or nightclubs. Maggie didn't want to be a hermit; she enjoyed socializing with her co-workers. But, her budget wasn't capable of supporting an extravagant social life. In order to continue going out with her friends, she decided to make a tradeoff. She decided to bring her lunch to work and redirect the money normally spent at her office's cafeteria to her entertainment budget. By being proactive,

Maggie found creative and practical solutions along her Prosperity Track.

Big-ticket items. Maggie kept her basic monthly expenses low by living with a roommate and driving an inexpensive car. She had a standard phone plan and basic cable TV. She didn't take extravagant trips to Las Vegas or Hawaii. She didn't buy a boat or a motorcycle. She avoided the temptation to buy the latest 3D television or the newest smartphone. However, she planned to reward herself with a new tablet computer once her student loans were paid off.

Credit cards. Maggie had one credit card she used infrequently for emergencies and paid off the balance every month. For her daily expenses, she used her debit card, and routinely checked her balance online. Maggie always knew whether she was honestly sticking to her plan.

While Maggie's plan was simple—to set aside a thousand dollars a month—it took determination to stay on the plan. Maggie was able to do it because she made a budget—just like you will do later—and she stuck to it. It helped that she *felt* more prosperous when following her plan. How is this possible? She felt increasingly prosperous because she was doing what she loved to do, and she didn't have daily worries over her bills. Maggie was in control of her life, and being in control is ninety percent of the battle. Her friends who were not on a plan constantly worried about their finances feverously, yet continued to overspend.

The Basic Economic Problem

We all face the same economic problem: we have *limited* resources and *unlimited* wants and needs. We have to match our resources to the most appropriate mix of needs and wants. Every choice we make will either eliminate or create an opportunity.

Remember Tony? As a suddenly rich reality TV star, he lived in an environment of seemingly limitless choices. The paparazzi photographed him wherever he went. His face was on magazine covers. Nightclub owners showered him with free drinks. He partied with celebrities and rock stars. Like the many impressionable young celebrities that came before him, this could have been the beginning of his demise.

But Tony understood the pain of poverty and was determined not to relive it. He knew the gravy train of reality TV show fame would soon come to an end, and the big fat paychecks would stop coming. Once that happened, the range of his choices would narrow sharply.

Tony objectively evaluated his resources and his choices. He asked himself, "What can I do to realistically make money and arrive at true prosperity?" He first cut his expenses by reducing his lavish lifestyle. He opted for a modest and affordable home in a quiet neighborhood. He hired a respected accountant and instructed the accountant to give him honest financial advice. Tony loved clothes and fashion, so he licensed his name to a reputable company and developed a clothing line.

What Tony did was *leverage* his assets—his assets being a brief influx of cash and his name recognition—into a lasting career. Leveraging is something everyone can do. Maggie leveraged her college degrees. Keith Richards leveraged his passion for music into a life-long career and great prosperity.

Here's another example of leveraging. In 1993, an immigrant from the United Kingdom named Joe Ades came to live with his daughter in Manhattan. He was fifty-nine years old and had no real skills except a knack for salesmanship. Ades bought a box of five-dollar vegetable peelers and sold them on the streets of Manhattan. He was good at it and he knew how to keep up a friendly dialogue with the passers-by. He made some money, invested the profits into more peelers, and then sold them on the street. Years later, he became so successful that he wore thousand-dollar suits, enjoyed the café society at the Pierre Hotel, and lived with his wife in a three-bedroom apartment on Park Avenue. He even became a celebrity and was profiled on TV and in magazines.

Joe Ades leveraged his modest opportunity into real prosperity. He began by making money five dollars at a time and didn't squander it. He kept his expenses low and his plan simple, yet enjoyed a prosperous lifestyle. His resources were initially limited but steady, and he didn't indulge in expensive things until he could afford to without getting off track.

Ten Principles

I'd like to present a set of ten basic principles that you should keep at the forefront of your prosperity journey.

1. ***Understand your income and expenses.*** You have a level of income, which can vary based on the choices you make. You have a combination of fixed and variable expenses. You must determine the mix best suited to make your vision of prosperity a reality.

2. ***Differentiate between needs and wants.*** There is an important difference between needs and wants. You must determine which wants to satisfy, and which ones to exclude. Life is about choices.

3. ***Prioritize.*** In order to reach your maximum potential, you must be able to prioritize. When everything is a priority, nothing is a priority.

4. ***Maintain records and track progress.*** It's imperative to keep records. When you write things down, it changes your behavior. By tracking your progress, you will see where you have been and where you are headed. This is apparent in many other aspects of life including work, nutrition, exercising, and sports.

5. ***Modify behavior.*** We each have a set of behavioral tendencies. We act a certain way and receive pleasure in different ways. In order to achieve prosperity you must understand your own behavior and its causes. By

understanding your behavior, you can make the adjustments needed to reach your greatest potential.

6. *Make tough decisions.* Life is a series of choices and many of them are difficult. Choose where you spend your time and money. You are at the helm, and your life is well within your control. Making the right choice is not always easy or popular. Before making an important decision, consider its effect on your vision of prosperity.

7. *Be proactive.* Prosperity takes planning. You must think ahead when making decisions. Many of your decisions have long-term consequences. Anticipate potential changes and plan for emergencies.

8. *Get started.* Although many people have great ideas, ideas alone mean very little. You must act. Getting started is the most important step. Without a start, there can be no finish.

9. *Have a long-term focus.* The road of prosperity can be long and winding, with no immediate grand results. Your plan must be long-term in nature.

10. *Celebrate successes.* Plan for indulgences to reward yourself. It's important to celebrate your successes in a way that does not derail your Prosperity Track. Rewards don't have to cost much money. Find activities that are special, memorable, and don't break the bank.

Shared Vision

Visualization is an important tool for achieving prosperity. By mentally picturing what your ideal prosperous life looks like, you can better work towards it. With a picture in mind, you can better decide whether something moves you toward or away from that picture.

Here is an example: Jim and Judy were newlyweds. They lived in a modest apartment in the city, and Jim had started his own website design business while Judy worked as a wedding consultant. They weren't living in poverty, but they didn't have many extras. They budgeted carefully and over time built up their savings account.

They owned one car, which they often took for weekend drives to the seashore. But they didn't just drive around aimlessly. Jim and Judy favored Pines Point, an exclusive area of town filled with historic houses, sprawling lawns, and big oak trees. Some of the houses had private docks, and in the driveways were parked sleek luxury vehicles. Jim and Judy would cruise through the neighborhood and discuss the houses they admired most. They'd talk about how they might paint this one a different color, or put a different set of shrubs on that one. As far as they were concerned, it was only a matter of time before they achieved their dream of owning a house in Pines Point. At home, they followed the real estate listings and learned about the home prices in Pines Point. At first, the prices seemed hopelessly out of reach. But as the years passed, Jim and Judy—despite now having two kids—were able to consistently save their money and increase their income. They vacationed at Jim's parents' house and didn't spend excessively. They didn't starve themselves or their kids; they just lived sensibly and well within their means.

Sure enough, after a few years they spotted a cozy three-bedroom home near the water in Pines Point. They contacted a realtor, toured the house, and got qualified for a mortgage. Three months after they first saw the house, and a few weeks shy of their fifth anniversary, Jim, Judy and their two kids moved into their new home in Pines Point. Through planning and dedication, what began as a dream was soon transformed into reality.

Getting Others Involved

When we tell others about our plans, we immediately become accountable. Fears of reprise or embarrassment help us stay on track. Others can also help as you progress. Sometimes it's hard to ask for help, but no one has ever become great without the help of someone else. Friends who know about your plan can support you in many ways.

When Roger opened his first restaurant, he knew he was in a tough business. Recent studies suggest that sixty percent of new restaurants fail in the first three years. Roger was determined not only to avoid failure, but to prosper.

Roger had experience in the restaurant business, but he didn't want to go it alone. Fortunately, his financial backer had invested in other restaurants, and could offer advice on everything from the layout to the menu and purchasing food. Together they formulated monthly budgets, constantly making adjustments and always looking for ways to increase efficiencies while providing superior service to their customers.

What helped Roger was that he was unafraid to have forthright conversations with his partner. They were in this together and honesty would be crucial to their success. At one point Roger discovered that bar costs were suddenly much too high. Instead of shrugging it off, Roger went to his partner and they discussed the possible causes, ranging from overpouring to employee theft. After talking to the staff, they were relieved to discover that their new bartender, who had come from another establishment, was simply pouring much bigger glasses of wine than the previous bartender. After a quick training session the operation was back on track.

Five years after Roger opened his first restaurant he noticed a failing restaurant nearby. He and his partner bought it and used their expertise to make it profitable. It was not long before Roger could consider himself not just successful but truly prosperous.

If you don't know someone who can help, there are many free resources to assist you along your journey. For mentoring services, many small business owners turn to the Service Corps of Retired Executives, now known simply as SCORE. It's a 501(c)(3) nonprofit organization that provides free business mentoring services to entrepreneurs in the United States. SCORE has approximately 370 chapters throughout the United States and its territories and thousands of volunteers.

Both active and retired business executives and entrepreneurs provide business mentoring services, donating their time and expertise as mentors to assist new and established small businesses. The organization also presents business workshops and seminars for a fee. "Ask SCORE" is the online counseling service. Visit www.score.org for more details.

Avoiding Entitlement

A feeling of entitlement will keep you from becoming prosperous. Entitled people believe the world owes them something. What has happened in the past is history and cannot be changed. Focus on the future and learn from your past experiences. When you expect nothing, you will never be disappointed. Sitting and waiting is boring and painful. Make it happen on your own.

Sharon was a young woman who was raised in a well-to-do family. Her parents weren't bad people; they just didn't provide their daughter with many practical tools for long-term prosperity. After her dad graduated from college, he waltzed into a plum job in a bank and had a lucrative career. But he started his career in the nineteen-sixties, and by the time his daughter was ready to enter the real world, times had changed.

When she graduated from college with an underwhelming C average, Sharon assumed all she had to do was send out a few resumes to her dad's contacts, and she could find a good job no problem. She did just that, but no one was hiring. She thought it was a minor setback, so she sent out a few more resumes. Still nothing. Then she started to panic. "Don't worry", her parents reassured her, "you come from a good family and you deserve a great career." But the world had different plans, and Sharon found herself at the bottom of the resume pile.

On a whim, Sharon decided to consult with an employment advisor. Maybe her resume could use some sprucing, she thought. When she went to see the advisor, she expected flattery and soothing words, but got a dose of tough love instead. The advisor told her the job market was intensely competitive and her C average, together with her lack of previous work experience at *any* job, was locking her out of the jobs for which she was applying.

How could Sharon solve this dilemma? The advisor asked Sharon what it was she really loved to do—what activity she would do, even if no one paid her to do it. It turned out Sharon loved animals. She had a pony when she was a kid, and always enjoyed visiting her uncle's farm and helping with the livestock. But her parents had always discouraged her from getting involved with animals professionally—it didn't seem to be a prestigious vocation.

The advisor told Sharon about an opening for an intern at the local animal rescue. It was unpaid, but they'd take her, and if it worked out, they might hire her full time. Meanwhile, the advisor told Sharon to take evening classes at the local community college in areas related to animal care. This would help improve her academic credentials.

Sharon's sense of entitlement almost destroyed her chances for lasting prosperity. But she decided to follow her heart and enter a profession she loved, even as an intern. After six months she was offered a full time job and went on to get her master's degree in animal science. Sharon made a plan for prosperity and followed it, achieving success and happiness.

Be True to Yourself

Your goals must be your own. Satisfaction begins with an understanding of what makes you happy. Unless you feel fulfilled, prosperity will continue to elude you.

Diego grew up in a family of achievers. His father was a surgeon and his older brother was a lawyer. When Diego was a senior in high school, his parents sat him down and told him that while playing tennis on the school team had been fun—the team had made it to the state semifinals—the idea of making a living playing tennis was foolish. His parents insisted Diego buckle down and choose a profession. By "profession" his parents meant law, medicine, or business. Tennis was deliberately absent from the list.

Diego was adamant. He chose a college with an outstanding tennis program and he made the starting team in his freshman year. Shortly after he graduated with a degree in sports management, he turned pro. His parents, who had initially stated their opposition to his career choice, eventually relented and even came to see him play. As a member of the professional tennis circuit, Diego saved his occasional winnings and learned about money management. After a few years, Diego came to grips with the fact he was never going to play at Wimbledon. He retired from professional tennis at the age of twenty-eight, and took a job as the director of tennis operations at an exclusive country club. A few years later, he opened his own tennis school and recruited some past players from the pro circuit to join his staff.

Under Diego's guidance, the school thrived and even produced a few world-class players. After experiencing financial success, Diego was able to dedicate much of his time to working with underprivileged children. He now had the time and resources to organize youth tennis workshops on the weekends and during the summer. He felt blessed with his success and felt compelled to pay it forward. Although he didn't get paid for his charitable work, the smiles he received were a more welcomed reward.

Keep Your Eye on the Prize

Visualize and continue to remind yourself what you are working for. Although you may not be there yet, you must always look towards your goal.

What better example could there be of focused determination than the sensational racecar driver Danica Patrick? Born March 25, 1982, Danica Patrick is the most successful woman in the history of American open-wheel racing. She's the only woman to win a race in the IndyCar Series and holds the highest finish (third place) by a woman at the Indianapolis 500. In 2013, she became the fastest pole qualifier for the Daytona 500 since 1990. She's also the first female NASCAR driver to win a NASCAR Sprint Cup Series pole, also at Daytona.

Born in Beloit, Wisconsin, she grew up in nearby Roscoe, Illinois. Her racing career began with go karting in 1992 at the age of ten at the Sugar River Raceway in Brodhead, Wisconsin. At age sixteen she moved to Milton Keynes, England to race in British national series events against top drivers. In order to pursue racing, she dropped out of high school, later earning her GED. During a three-year period in the U.K., she raced in Formula Ford, Formula Vauxhall and earned a second-place finish in Britain's Formula Ford Festival, the highest finish by an American in the event. In 2002, Danica started driving for Rahal Letterman Racing in the United States and quickly became a media and track sensation.

Auto racing is highly competitive no matter who you are, but what makes Danica exceptional is that auto racing is traditionally a men's sport, and there are only a few women drivers. Danica Patrick had to constantly battle to be taken seriously, and a big part of her success has been her ability to keep her eye on the prize. As you make your way along the long road of prosperity, you'll find there are obstacles and temptations, and it's easy to get sidetracked. Stay focused and stay on track!

Chapter Two Takeaways

Becoming prosperous requires vision, execution, and discipline. By understanding what brings you joy and contentment, you can visualize your prosperous lifestyle. Your vision of prosperity will help guide you along the Prosperity Track. When faced with a decision, you should consider the potential ramifications relative to your vision. Does your decision get you closer or farther from prosperity? Your greatest chance for achieving prosperity lies within your ability to maintain control of your own actions. You may need to learn new skills or enlist others to help you along your journey. Commit to your vision of prosperity, and everything else will begin falling into place.

Prosperity in Practice

How do you envision prosperity?

What will you be doing?

What will you no longer be doing?

What brings you the most happiness?

Who can help you along your journey?

Who or what are negative influences?

Chapter Three
Your Current Position

When you find yourself in a hole, the first thing to do is stop digging.

Tammara Webber

In Chapters One and Two, I revealed the first two steps towards achieving prosperity. The first step was to define prosperity and build an image of a prosperous life in your mind. You cannot achieve a goal without knowing where it is and what it looks like! There will be many challenges and distractions along the road of prosperity, and you need to keep your "eye on the prize." In Chapter Two we laid the foundation for your eventual prosperity. We discussed what it takes to become prosperous, and I provided several examples—some featuring well-known celebrities and others with regular folks just like you and me—of people who had overcome challenges to enjoy a prosperous lifestyle. It's important to recognize that prosperity is relative to your own vision. Remember our definition of prosperity:

The personal state of achievement, contentment, and wellbeing.

There is no dollar sign attached to this definition. Many people are prosperous who own modest material possessions. I know of a man who lives in a small cabin in the woods of Oregon. He could pack everything he owns into the back of his old pickup truck. But he owns his cabin and his land—a tract that affords him a breathtaking view of the mountains—and he wants for nothing. He's as happy as any human being on earth, because he aligned his vision of prosperity with his resources and expectations. His modest income exceeds his expenses and he goes to bed each night with a satisfied smile on his face.

Of course he's an exception; most of us aspire to take part in social activities, travel, and have hobbies. To be blunt, we need a little more cash flow than a man living in a cabin in the woods. And that's fine. The goal is to not arrive at some dollar figure, or to say, "I will be prosperous when I have a million dollars in the bank." That's irrelevant. It's more important to be on the road of prosperity than to give it a dollar figure, because once you near your dollar goal, you'd probably raise your goal anyway! The person who aspires to own a yacht and buys one, will eventually want to trade up to a bigger one. Whether he or she can successfully do so depends on their level of wealth, not prosperity. The question remains, "Will this make them happy?"

In Chapter Three, I'll take you farther on your journey. In order to start on the Prosperity Track, you need to know two things: where you want to go and where you are now. Earlier, you began developing your vision of prosperity, and now we must examine your current position. Knowing your current position is extremely important. By being honest with yourself and knowing where you are, you'll learn how far you have to go before feeling the benefits of a prosperous life.

Charles was a bright young man who aspired to a life of prosperity. He had a good job and had some basic money management skills. A person like Charles should have a fruitful journey reaping the benefits of a prosperous life—security, satisfaction, and financial freedom. But unfortunately, Charles never felt secure. He couldn't pay his bills and even had collection agencies calling him. The money he earned just seemed to disappear without a trace. Charles wanted to move out of his apartment and buy a house, but he couldn't qualify for a mortgage. The banks told him he was high risk due to his low credit score and his high debt-to-income ratio.

Charles's problem wasn't that he was lazy, wasn't good at his job, or was a bad person. What held Charles back was that he was unwilling to take a hard look at his current position. He succumbed to temptation easily and often. He enjoyed going with friends to nightclubs and restaurants and often spent freely. Every two to three years he leased a different luxury car, each time leasing a more expensive model (it's much cheaper to buy a good car, pay off the auto loan, and then keep it a few more years). Charles also took lavish vacations to five-star Caribbean resorts during peak seasons. These things aren't bad as long as you can pay for them *and* stay on the Prosperity Track. But Charles used credit cards and was habitually late making his monthly payments. He paid high interest rates due to his high-risk behavior, and eventually maxed out his credit lines. When it was all said and done, Charles had a mountain of debt and nothing to show for it.

Fortunately for Charles, the thrill of luxury consumption grew tiresome compared to the price he was paying, and he decided to get serious about achieving prosperity. After taking stock of his finances, he cut back his spending and eventually paid off his credit cards. Once his debt levels improved, his credit rating strengthened and he was able to qualify for a mortgage. He bought a reasonably priced house and hasn't looked back since. And there was a side benefit he hadn't anticipated—he felt better and even looked better. His friends and co-workers noticed the positive change in his attitude and appearance. He shared his story freely and was able to help some close friends and co-workers with their dangerous spending.

In order to get on the Prosperity Track, you must objectively analyze your current position. Only by doing this will you know how far you have to go to live the prosperous life. It may also take some effort to understand why you behave the way you do. There may be deep-rooted explanations that expand far beyond the scope of this book. Many times, we do things in order to feel a certain way, other times to not feel a certain way. These choices have led us to where we are today. That's why it's important to be realistic about your position as it exists right now, not last year, or ten years ago. Although it's important to look towards tomorrow, please avoid spending tomorrow's income today.

Unfortunately, many people spend their future income before it's earned. Some people do so with annual bonuses, tax returns, and inheritances. This is a trap! You don't know what is going to happen tomorrow and that includes the aforementioned cash influxes. Be responsible with the money you have now. Spending tomorrow's dollar is a dangerous habit that has been detrimental to many a person's prosperity. Another activity detrimental to prosperity is the use of payday loans.

Payday loans, which often carry interest rates in excess of 100% annually, are used to keep you afloat for a short time. People using payday loans are typically shortsighted in their financial planning. They live paycheck to paycheck and rarely plan for the future. What originally began as a short-term fix, can result in a vicious circle of spend, borrow, payoff, spend, borrow, payoff, repeat...

Life Stages

Let's look at some of the stages people experience. Where are you in your life? You may be:

Twenty years old and a high school graduate who's already in the work force. You may have low expenses and even live at home with your parents. You have an incredible opportunity to save your money, but you're also at a stage in life when the temptations to spend money are powerful. You may want to acquire a new car, buy the newest electronic gadget, hang out with your friends, and generally do everything except plan for the future. To a twenty-year-old, the idea of life in middle age is about as believable as life on the planet Mars. Young people tend to live in the moment, and the idea of their money just sitting in the bank unused seems silly. If you've got it, you want to spend it! It takes great fortitude for a young person to take a long view and plan for a life of prosperity, but it can be done.

In your mid-twenties and just out of college. You have a job but you likely have student loan debt. At this stage, some of life's hard realities are part of your personal experience. You know how much college has cost you and you realize how competitive the job market is. If you have an apartment, you may need a roommate to make ends meet. Your expenses include your cell phone, transportation (a car or your subway pass), clothes, health insurance, rent, and of course your student loan debt. It may be difficult to pay for all of this stuff on your entry-level salary or hourly wage.

An entrepreneur with a new business. Take all the stress factors in the previous section and add the fact that you're starting your own business. This means that you're working ridiculously long hours and if you make a mistake, it comes out of your pocket. You might even be sleeping on the floor of your new business! It's challenging, but you may be closer to living a life of sustained prosperity than you think.

Starting a new family. Not only do you have yourself to think of, but your kids and your partner as well. Naturally, you'll want to live in a safe neighborhood with good schools, and you may want to buy a house in the suburbs. Everything seems to cost more, and there are more things to pay for than before—day care, toys, clothes, etc. In families with two wage earners, sometimes the lower-paid partner's entire earnings go to pay for child care. The early years are a financial challenge, but you can still lay the groundwork for long-term prosperity.

In mid-career, nearing the peak of your earning potential. You may be paying your children's college expenses while putting real thought into your retirement. And let's face it: you have powerful impulses to spend your money. Your friends and colleagues are at the height of their earning power too, and they're buying fancier cars, taking exotic vacations, buying second homes, and generally living large. So while your paycheck may be getting larger, so too are your expenses. This phenomenon is referred to as "lifestyle inflation."

As your income grows, your lifestyle grows at the same pace. It's at this time a catastrophe such as a job layoff or major medical problem can wreak havoc with your plans for prosperity. In fact, a recent study[1] indicated that the biggest single cause of bankruptcy is unexpected medical expenses, representing sixty-two percent of all personal bankruptcies. Serious diseases or injuries can easily result in hundreds of thousands of dollars in medical bills that can quickly wipe out savings and retirement accounts, college education funds,

---

[1] Medical Bankruptcy in the United States, 2007: Results of a National Study
David U. Himmelstein, MD,[a] Deborah Thorne, PhD,[b] Elizabeth Warren, JD,[c] Steffie Woolhandler, MD, MPH[a]

and home equity. Other leading causes of mid-career bankruptcy are job loss, divorce, natural disaster, and overuse of credit cards. You can't avoid all of these challenges, but you can plan ahead for emergencies.

Nearing retirement. This is the stage when you have reached your earnings peak, and may be worrying it's too late to build up your retirement fund. Medical expenses may increase, and you may consider selling your house and using the equity to fund your retirement. If you work at a large organization you may face mandatory retirement age; if you're self-employed, you may wonder *when* you'll be able to retire! No one wants to retire without the resources for a comfortable life. Prosperity requires good planning. Consider it your second act in life. If you retire from your job, that doesn't mean you can't generate income. Many people nearing retirement identify new income streams to help them transition into retirement more easily. An additional income stream can supplement social security and pension benefits, while creating less drag on your savings.

It doesn't matter where you are in life, you can make a positive impact. It will take effort and work, but you can do it. If you are young, you may need to get some formalized training. If you are mid-career, you may have to get out of your comfort zone. Fear is a strong emotion and can be crippling. However, the feeling of accomplishment is even stronger. If you are at a more advanced stage, you may have to try things you don't think you can accomplish. It will be uncomfortable, but it's worth it. The bigger the reward, the bigger the sacrifice and effort required to achieve it. Many people believe you can't teach an old dog new tricks, but luckily, *you* can learn new things!

Your Current State

To embark on the Prosperity Track, you need to know where you are now. Let's begin by establishing some broad characteristics. You can answer these questions in your head, or you can write them down. Whatever works for you is just fine. The goal is to take action! Remember there are no right or wrong answers. You may be frugal or a spender. You may be flush with cash or continuously looking under the sofa cushions for spare change. You may keep meticulous financial records or just throw your receipts into a shoebox. Wherever you are in your journey to prosperity, it's okay—you can always get on the track and move ahead. You have the power to change, but it will take effort and discipline. With focus and commitment, your optimal prosperous life is well within your grasp.

Attitude – What type of person are you? Are you inherently optimistic and believe in a better future, or are you more pessimistic and believe your best days are behind you? Do you have clear goals in life, or do you live one day at a time? Are you able to manage your finances on your own, or do you need help?

Rob and Megan were a happily married couple with two wonderful kids. They lived in a nice house and owned two cars. Both Rob and Megan worked—he was an electrician and she was a teacher—and you'd think they would have little problem achieving prosperity. But year after year they barely scraped by! There never seemed to be enough money for anything extra, and they always seemed to be barely treading water financially. Based on the recommendation from their accountant, they met with a financial advisor. After a candid session of self-examination, the cause of the problem surfaced. Rob managed the family's finances, which he did by default. His dad had managed the family finances, and when Rob and Megan were first married, Rob assumed the job of family finance manager. He paid the bills and kept track of the bank accounts and credit cards. Megan welcomed this arrangement because she believed it pleased Rob, and it happened without any real discussion. It was just assumed Rob would handle the family's financial affairs, as his father did.

With the help of the advisor, Rob and Megan made a startling discovery: Rob dreaded handling financial matters and subconsciously avoided paying bills. He was a highly skilled electrician but a lousy financial manager. He had assumed the role merely because his dad had done it and it seemed like a logical fit.

Rob was relieved when Megan took over the family finances. He never really enjoyed the job, whereas his wife threw herself into it with enthusiasm. She actually enjoyed being responsible for managing the family's finances. It was not long before she made some important changes that got the family on a solid track to prosperity. The interesting thing was their lifestyle didn't change much—just a little trim here and there. The big change was their peace of mind.

They had fewer fights and even the kids noticed the household was more relaxed and happy. It wasn't long before they had healthy retirement accounts and even extra money for a vacation.

Are you like Rob or Megan? There's no shame in being like Rob; he was a good provider and a great father to his kids. But when it came to managing money, it took him a long time to admit to himself and to his wife he didn't have the knowhow to guide his family along the road of prosperity.

Financial – As we saw from the example above, Rob and Megan didn't have an income problem preventing them from achieving prosperity. They made enough money; the challenge was it wasn't being managed effectively.

For others, it's a matter of having insufficient income to meet household expenses. Take a quick look at your finances. Use a simple chart and list your monthly expenses. Make the list fairly general; we'll do this in greater detail later. Add up your rent/mortgage, taxes, utilities, retirement contribution, car payments, insurance, health plan costs, and loan obligations. You pay these fixed expenses every month. Unless you make a change in your lifestyle, such as trading in your big SUV for a less expensive car, these payments are not likely to change in the short-term. They can and will change in the long-term as you pay off your car loan and keep the car you now own free and clear, pay down credit cards, and perhaps take steps to make your home more energy efficient.

The next category of expense consists of the daily expenses related to your physical survival. I'm talking about food, money for gas to drive to work or for your subway pass, and medical expenses. These costs probably remain consistent week after week. But you can lower them by being a smart shopper and comparing prices before going to the store. Many shoppers also realize significant savings when they buy items in bulk.

The third category of expense is the one that requires total honesty, because it's here you're most likely to underestimate. This category includes all the stuff you buy that's nonessential. It's the morning gourmet coffee on the way to work, the afternoon pastry, entertainment, eating out at restaurants, buying clothes you don't need, lottery tickets, the super deluxe cable TV package, gourmet foods at the grocery store, and things like cigarettes (if you smoke, please quit—it's bad for your health, and it's insanely expensive). Be honest when you estimate these expenses, because collectively they're probably much higher than you'd expect. These costs can be cut down immediately.

Now calculate your monthly income. Include wages, Social Security benefits, alimony, dividends, interest, distributions, etc. If you have complicated income from several sources, you can refer to last year's tax returns to give you a realistic figure.

Then compare your expenses with your income. To begin feeling prosperous, your income needs to be greater than your expenses. If your income is lower than your expenses, chances are you're borrowing to make up the difference. The most common way consumers borrow money is by using a credit card, which is merely an expensive credit line. These loans can carry interest rates of twenty percent or more, so unless you're using a credit card for real emergencies or you're paying off the balance in full every month, it makes little sense wasting your money on credit card interest. I am confident you can find a better way to spend your hard-earned money.

And if you need to use payday loans to make it through the month, you really need to bring your income and expenses into balance. Payday loans are incredibly expensive and must be avoided at all costs. If you are consistently using revolving or short-term credit solutions to finance your lifestyle, you need to seriously adjust your spending. In drastic cases, such as these, drastic actions and remedies are required.

Take Miranda for example. She was a single woman living in the city. She was perfectly capable of balancing her checkbook and her monthly nonessential expenses were not excessive. Yet month after month, she barely scraped by, and after she had paid her rent she was nearly broke until her next payday. She thought she was frugal, but her income of $3,500 a month never seemed adequate.

The main problem was her rent. Experts agree that no more than 28% of your income should go towards housing, including heat and water. Miranda had signed a lease for a two-bedroom apartment that cost a whopping $1,500 a month. For a few months, she sublet the second bedroom to a girlfriend for $500 a month, but the girlfriend moved out and Miranda's boyfriend moved in. But the guy wasn't paying rent! Miranda found herself shouldering the entire burden of the rent, and it was costing her 43% of her monthly income—nearly half. It was no wonder that after paying her landlord, she was broke.

Miranda faced a difficult decision. After a heart-to-heart discussion with her freeloading boyfriend, he decided to find accommodations elsewhere. It would have been wonderful if he had stepped up and taken responsibility, but he didn't, and it was a clear signal to Miranda that she needed to make a tough choice. Miranda sublet the room to a co-worker and was quickly back on the Prosperity Track.

Spiritual – Your attitudes towards wealth and prosperity can have an impact on your dedication to managing your budget. Do you feel a moral obligation to repay debt?

Some religions, such as the Amish, are noted for their conservative approach to debt. For the Amish, debt is just another tool. Some Amish even use credit cards. It's a minority, but those who use credit cards do so only for the sake of convenience. The Amish have a moral obligation to repay their debts on time and in full. This means Amish consumers are unlikely to carry large credit card balances like many other Americans do. They use credit cards to make life easier, not to spend beyond one's means.

The Amish commonly use bank credit for home mortgages or to fund businesses. Like many other business owners, bank credit helps them operate and expand. Also, they consider a reasonable amount of debt to be powerful motivation. Having something to pay back keeps you motivated; so the right type of debt can be healthy. The Amish embody hard work and determination, and consequently enjoy a solid reputation in the banking community.

But why are the Amish exemplary when it comes to credit and debt? It's a combination of their cultural tradition, the feelings of disgrace that would befall a member of the community who lapsed, and the support offered by the community towards members who need help.

Responsible financial management is also an important focus of Mormon teachings. Lessons of responsible spending, debt avoidance, budgeting, the importance of hard work, and establishing an emergency fund are engrained in their religion. Many Mormons believe that money matters should be discussed with children early, using examples they can understand. Certain faiths consider financial matters to be such an important aspect of family life that couples wishing to get married are encouraged to discuss financial matters in detail prior to marriage.

Regardless of your spiritual or religious views, I believe you will agree that budgeting, prudent spending, and a low reliance on debt are important lessons.

Howard was a retiree who lived a comfortable life on an income of $4,000 a month. If he had stuck to his budget, he could have lived a long time without financial worry. He drove an economy car, lived modestly, and felt he was careful with his spending.

He was responsible with his money until the moment he boarded the bus at the senior center for the weekly casino trip.

With a busload of friends at the casino, Howard's good judgment went out the window. He played slots and the roulette wheel, and although he won a few jackpots, he usually lost a thousand dollars or more per month. But he thought nothing of it because everybody else was doing it and it was fun.

His daughter, who talked to him about his finances every now and then, began hearing stories of her father's gambling losses. She knew his fixed income could not support those losses every month. At the rate he was going, he could have real financial problems very soon. Her dad was stubborn and she knew he wasn't going to listen to her. Luckily, Howard did have a friendly relationship with the pastor of his church, so she asked her dad to have a talk with him. They did, and after the discussion, Howard learned how to go on the senior citizen bus rides to the casino, have fun with his friends, and stick to a firm budget when playing the games. For all future casino trips, Howard modified his behavior—he only took what he afforded himself to lose and left his ATM card at home. A financial disaster was averted and Howard was back on the Prosperity Track.

Emotional – For many people, the emotional element is the biggest challenge of all. How do you feel when you spend money? Is the thrill of an acquisition soon eclipsed by a sense of guilt you spent too much money? Do you buy clothes only to put them in your closet and never wear them? Is available credit on your credit card too tempting? If so, you may very well have an emotional attachment to spending money.

Here are five key reasons why people overspend for emotional reasons:

1. *To feel happy.* Many people derive pleasure from buying things. They spend large sums of money when they are sad, depressed, or lonely. Sales people are usually very nice; they

listen to us and cater to our egos. There is no doubt why this is referred to as "retail therapy." Unfortunately, this happiness is only a temporary reprieve from the source of negative feelings. Once the excitement of shopping has passed, the guilt experienced afterwards can make us feel even worse.

2. *To maintain our image.* This type of behavior is commonly referred to as "keeping up with the Joneses." We all care what other people think of us and no one wants to feel inferior. We sometimes buy things to show we can afford those things too. While this behavior might not make us happy, it may help alleviate a feeling of inferiority.

3. *To impress others.* We want to appear successful. We sometimes buy expensive things to make other people envious. We want others to see we own expensive things like designer clothes, luxury cars, and big houses. Unfortunately, we sometimes buy things we don't need, with money we don't have, to impress people who don't matter.

4. *Entitlement.* People often buy things because they "deserve it." This behavior is fine, if the spending occurs within your designated budget. However, changes in income, wealth, or circumstances may require a more modest standard of living. Many spenders assert that any expenses incurred to maintain their customary lifestyle are justified.

5. *To overcome a painful past.* If you experienced a financially troubled childhood, it's normal for those feelings to impact future decisions. Be careful, these feelings can be excessively

strong. The key is to not overcompensate or "make up for lost time" spending money that derails your prosperity.

Should you find yourself engaging in emotional spending, you owe it to yourself to recognize the issue and take steps to control it. Hold yourself accountable for your spending. The people you live with or spend the most time with can be supportive allies. Let them know you're trying to cut your needless spending, and you want them to tell you when they see you making an unnecessary purchase. It may help if everyone in your group makes the same pledge, because it's often easier to accomplish a change in behavior when your friends and family are participating too.

I once met a guy who put his credit card in a plastic container of water, and put the container in the freezer. In order to use his credit card, he had to plan ahead and thaw it out. This helped him eliminate impulse purchases.

If you frequently use shopping as a distraction or form of entertainment, identify how you feel when you have the urge to buy something, then find a more constructive activity that will help you sidestep that emotion. For example, if you're feeling stressed out, get some exercise instead of going shopping. If you've had a bad day at work and want to indulge in some retail therapy, call a friend or two and go have coffee. If you really must buy something, make it something that will improve your life, like a book or music. But be careful; those small purchases can really add up.

Life Clutter

All of us come with a lifetime of baggage. Some of us have a carry-on, while others have the matched set with the full trunk. Hard decisions may be required in order to de-clutter one's life. This could involve people, attachments, or possessions.

It would probably amaze you to go through your house and identify all the stuff you haven't used and probably never will use. I know a guy who brought his old lawnmower with him when he moved from a house into a condominium. He said, "Well, you never know when you might need a lawnmower." He kept the darned thing in the condo storage area, constantly bumping into it or having to move it. After three years of cluttering up his storage unit, he finally put it out on the sidewalk with a big "FREE" sign on it. The next morning it was gone—taken to a home where it could be put to good use. If you have unwanted items, you can donate them, sell them, or give them away. It's up to you to decide the best course of action to clean up your life.

There's financial clutter too. If you have a mortgage, check to see if you can refinance at a lower fixed rate. You may have signed your mortgage years ago and are unknowingly paying a much higher rate than you need to.

Many people have automatic recurring payments that are applied to their bank account or credit card unnoticed. Once a month you should carefully review your bank and credit card statements and look for any unusual or recurring debits. If you find one—an old online subscription service for example—cancel it immediately. Your bank will probably allow you to dispute the charge; call them and tell them you want to stop the charges.

Debt Management

A discussion about debt is critical for understanding your current condition and forming a plan for the future. It's important to recognize the debt you have and make a plan to eliminate it. The physical and emotional strain caused by debt can be debilitating. Entire books have been written on the subject of debt management. For the purposes of the Prosperity Track, you need to understand the debt you have, be smarter about borrowing money in the future, and implement a debt elimination plan. We will begin our discussion by examining how debt is accumulated.

People accumulate debt for a number of reasons. Sometimes the reasons make sense at the time, but look differently later in life. Debt is used for two main reasons: to buy things you can't afford to pay for all at once, or to utilize leverage. The former is the most common. We typically borrow money in order to finance expensive purchases, spreading the payments out over several months or even years. The more expensive the item, the longer the payment period. While a new television may have a twelve month finance period, a home can be financed over the course of thirty years. The longer the payment period, the smaller the monthly payment, but the more interest you will pay overall. The second reason, utilizing leverage is commonly associated with investment decisions. Rather than sell property or investments earning a return, the person chooses to borrow money. The idea is that the cost of borrowing will be less than the rate of return for investing. Unfortunately, this is not always the case. Many investors underestimate the expected risk and return of investments, leaving only a small margin of error.

Debt itself is neither bad nor good. It all depends on the reason for borrowing. Reasonable borrowing for advanced education, a home, or an automobile is quite common. These are the most expensive items we pay for and typically require a multi-year payment program. Luckily, these types of loans have multi-year benefits. As a rule, the payment period should be significantly shorter than the useful life of the purchase. Stated alternatively, you never want to be making payments for something that no longer benefits you. Another rule is if you cannot afford to buy the item immediately, question whether you need it at all. Ponder what would happen if you were unable to borrow the money to buy the item. How would your life be different? Would you feel differently? How long would you have to save to buy it instead of borrowing? By saving over time, how much money would you save in interest?

Never use a short-term solution to solve a long-term problem. People often get into trouble with debt due to long-term problems. I know several people that continue to borrow from family members to pay their bills. If temporary trouble befalls you, this scenario is understandable. However, most cases result from an imbalance of income and spending, which is a long-term problem. Some people who borrow money from family or friends "temporarily", find themselves in the same predicament just a few months later. Unless behavior is modified, the cycle will continue.

Another example of a short-term solution addressing a long-term problem is the use of credit cards. Credit cards enable people to consistently overspend until they reach their borrowing limit. This has been a growing epidemic in recent years. Excessive credit card balances is the most common financial problem of Americans today. Credit cards are the most dangerous type of debt for several reasons:

High interest rates. Unlike a home or auto loan, credit cards do not have pledged collateral. If you don't pay your mortgage or car loan, the bank takes back ownership of the property or vehicle. This reduces the banks' risk of loss. Credit cards rarely have collateral and it can be difficult to recover property from borrowers. This high risk of uncollectable debt requires a higher amount of interest to entice banks to lend.

High fees. Credit cards have many different types of fees. Some cards have an annual fee simply for the privilege of using the card. Credit cards also have fees and penalties for late payments and for exceeding your credit limit. Americans spend billions of dollars every year on unnecessary credit card fees.

Low minimum payments. Most banks only require a minimum monthly payment of 2% of your monthly balance. Because of the high interest rates charged by credit card companies, paying the minimum due will only pay the monthly interest. Unfortunately, by making the minimum payment, you are only keeping your balance from getting bigger and not significantly reducing the balance. For example, a credit card with a balance of $10,000 and an 18% interest rate would have a monthly payment of $200. After you made your $200 payment, your balance would still be $9,950. Although you may be able to afford a $200 monthly payment, you would have to make that same payment for almost eight years to pay off the debt! After 94 month of payments, you will have spent a total of $18,622.36, almost twice the original amount.

Psychological factors. Swiping a credit card can be a much different mental experience than paying with cash or using a debit card. Mathematically it may be the same, but mentally we process these transactions differently. The use of cash and debit cards are easily accountable in our minds. We know the cash has left our wallet or purse, never to return. Most people account for the debit card transactions in order to avoid overdrawing their account. A credit card is different, since the payment may not be due for a month or more. Also, using a credit card may not immediately affect your spending on other things. It can be alarming to learn that most people with high credit card balances have a hard time explaining where the debt came from. Large balances tend to result from many small purchases that have accumulated over time.

Know Your Debt

It is important that you understand your debt intimately. You need to know the terms, interest rates, payment amounts, payment periods, penalties, fees, etc. These factors can determine which debt you pay off first and which you keep the longest. Many people don't realize there are early termination fees or penalty interest rates until it's too late. If you have questions, call the bank and ask for documentation. Borrowing often involves a monstrous amount of paperwork. There can be covenants or agreements you are unaware of. Before considering a debt refinance or payoff, discuss the scenario with the lender.

If you have loans outstanding, periodically call the bank and see if they have any promotional offers or opportunities to save money. Call your credit card company and ask for a rate reduction. If the first person does not have the ability or the authority to assist you, speak to their supervisor or manager. The worst thing that can happen is they say "no."

Once you have a firm understanding of your debt and its applicable terms, you can formulate a plan to reduce your debt. After paying off credit cards and student loans, people often feel a sense of relief and accomplishment. Their attitude improves, and they feel as if a large weight has been lifted off their shoulders. Great flexibility and wellbeing can be achieved through proper debt management. I urge you to collect your debt information as you will need it to complete some forthcoming worksheets.

Tools

Tools will help you paint an accurate financial picture. Visit www.prosperitytrack.com/tools for links and samples. Here are some tools that can help you budget; they range from online to electronic to good ol' fashioned paper and pencil:

- *Mint.com* – Excellent tool for collecting and also for tracking financial information from a variety of sources. It's very secure and efficient for tracking spending and balances.
- *Quicken* – Another good tool for bill pay, and tracking income and expenses.
- *Spreadsheet* – Keeping track via Microsoft Excel. This program is very customizable.
- *Legal pads* – Old school, but effective.
- *Notebooks/Binders* – Inexpensive and easy to keep information in chronological order.
- *Journals* – Important for recording feelings and mental awareness.
- *Calendar* – For tracking goals, progress, due dates, etc.

Worksheets

It is important to keep an accurate accounting of your financial condition. This will help later when we discuss goals and planning. Detailed explanations and images of the worksheets can be found in the *Worksheets* section at the end of the book. Visit www.prosperitytrack.com/tools to view and download the following worksheets:

Budget Timeline – Begin tracking all of your income and expenditures. It is important to understand exactly what comes in and what goes out of your accounts. Look for patterns in spending and account balances. Are there days in the month where you have to use money from your savings account or a credit card? Accurate budgeting can only be accomplished when you know precisely what you make and what you spend. This exercise should be completed monthly for the next three months.

Budget Worksheet – Prosperity requires you to be proactive in making life decisions, which includes spending. Create spending targets at the beginning of each month and then review at the end of the month. Set a budget each month and see where you spent more or less. When budgeting, we often underestimate how much money we really spend. Depending on your current position, you may complete this worksheet on a weekly basis early in the process. Tracking your income and expenses weekly will keep you focused on setting an appropriate budget and sticking to it. Eventually, you will move to biweekly and then monthly budgeting. Complete this exercise for the next three months.

Personal Balance Sheet – It is important to understand your assets and liabilities. By knowing what you have and what you owe, you are able to make better decisions. Most people never take a holistic look at their condition. Track your level of assets and your level of liabilities. Are they going up or are they going down? Look for trends in the amount of debt and savings you have. Your goal should be to consistently increase your net worth. By keeping an accurate record of your assets and liabilities, you can see your debt decrease and assets increase over time. Seeing improvement on your *Personal Balance Sheet* can be powerful motivation. This exercise is crucial for staying on the Prosperity Track. Initially you will do this monthly and eventually move to quarterly reporting.

Staying on Track

No matter how you do it, the key is to boldly put down *in writing* your expenses and your income. I'll repeat what I said earlier, which is that your income must be more than your total expenses. Ideally, you should save 10% of your net income. This means that if your monthly take home pay is $4,500, then your expenses should be no more than $4,500 – 10% = $4,050. Make that an even $4,000, which means that each month you should have an extra $500 to save or invest. If you invest $500 a month, at the end of the year you will have invested $6,000. That's a sweet little nest egg!

Don't count your tax refund as part of your household budget. If you get a tax refund, consider it "found" money and save it, invest it, or pay down debt. Be careful not to spend money before you receive it. Many people fall into the trap of "spending the same dollar twice." They use their credit cards or store credit lines to purchase items they intend to pay off with a future cash inflow. Unfortunately, most people overspend the expected cash inflow and in many cases overshoot by 100%!

Dan and Martha had two great kids and a home in the suburbs. He worked as a teacher and she worked in retail, and together they took home $80,000 a year. They weren't wealthy but they managed their money well and managed to save and invest close to $8,000 a year. They were on the road of prosperity.

When their eldest child reached college age, they thought they were prepared. But when Martha's mom passed away, her dad had to move in with them. Her mom and dad had almost no savings, but what was more challenging was her dad had Alzheimer's and needed an ever-increasing level of personal care. Martha had to cut back her hours at a time when the family needed more income, not less. They were concerned they couldn't help their eldest child pay for college—even state universities are becoming very expensive—and their younger child was entering high school. He was very athletic, which meant the family had to pay steep athletic activity fees in addition to the normal expenses growing kids require.

When Dan and Martha were late with a mortgage payment—the first time it had ever happened—they realized their dream of prosperity was suddenly slipping away.

They sat down and made a detailed family budget. There wasn't much they could do to increase their income except to find state assistance for Martha's dad, allowing her to take more hours at the store. They cut back on many of their nonessential expenses such as premium cable, and they sold their timeshare island vacation condo. Dan's car payments were ending and he opted to keep his car rather than buy a new one, meanwhile Martha changed her shopping habits and was more mindful of the family budget.

By taking a realistic look at their current position, and letting go some comforts they had enjoyed in the past, Dan and Martha were able to make the necessary changes and get back on the Prosperity Track.

Chapter Three Takeaways

Without a realistic view of your current position, you cannot progress along the Prosperity Track. Only after you know where you are, can you begin to formulate a plan for where you want to go. It doesn't matter where you are today, prosperity will be in your future only if you take action. By analyzing your current position, you may better understand your behavioral tendencies. There are many tools available to help you along your journey, find what works best for you. Take the time to create a budget before each month and examine the results after the month. This will be your guide for budgeting the following month. By keeping track of your current state, you will be able to compare your status later on, witnessing the improvement in your condition. These positive changes can help motivate you in the future.

> ## *Prosperity in Practice*
>
> *What life stage are you in now?*
>
> *How does your current stage help you?*
>
> *Where can you improve your prosperity?*
>
> *How can you improve your prosperity?*

Prosperity in Action

Use the Budget Timeline Worksheet to track all of your income and expenses for the next three months. Evaluate each budget item and determine if it is consistent with your vision of prosperity.

Use the Budget Worksheet to develop a monthly budget prior to the beginning of each of the next three months. Analyze your budget results at the end of each month to see where you deviated or were accurate. Use this information to make a more appropriate budget for the next month.

Complete a Personal Balance Sheet monthly for the next three months. Determine whether you are consistently increasing or decreasing your net worth. Examine areas responsible for changes. Investigate whether your financial position is in line with your vision of prosperity.

Chapter Four

Prosperity Goals

"Cat: Where are you going?
Alice: Which way should I go?
Cat: That depends on where you are going.
Alice: I don't know.
Cat: Then it doesn't matter which way you go."
Lewis Carroll, Alice in Wonderland

Let's review our progress thus far. In Chapters One and Two, I revealed the first two steps towards achieving prosperity. The first step was to define prosperity and build an image of a prosperous life in your mind. The second step was to lay the foundation for your eventual prosperity. We discussed what it takes to become prosperous, and I provided examples of people who had overcome challenges to enjoy a prosperous lifestyle. I also revealed our definition of prosperity, which guides our journey every step of the way. Prosperity is:

The personal state of achievement, contentment, and wellbeing.

The goal of the Prosperity Track is not to arrive at some specific dollar target, but to define what your life will look like. It's more important to be on the road of prosperity than to actually assign it a dollar figure. True prosperity is not about constantly striving for more money. Prosperity is about living a fulfilled life, long before reaching retirement. Enjoy the journey; it's more important than the destination.

In Chapter Three, we evaluated where you are *now*. You can't start on the Prosperity Track without knowing where you are today. Only by being honest with yourself and understanding your present condition will you know how far you have to go to achieve a prosperous life.

Now that you have a concrete understanding of where you are, you are able to move forward and define some specific goals. We'll do this in Chapter Four.

Prosperity is a process and not a destination, so we need to set and achieve specific goals in order to stay on the Prosperity Track. It's like driving on the highway—we need the lines between the lanes, the signs, and the guardrails to help us stay on the road and moving forward. These tools facilitate our progress and guide us along our journey. Without these tools, we would be forever lost.

Goals are important tools for reaching prosperity. It's easier to create a plan for accomplishing a long-term objective like prosperity by setting specific goals. It has been said that those failing to plan are in fact planning to fail. By setting a series of specific goals, you are able to determine whether your actions are getting you closer to your overall goal or keeping you from it. Many times, people set goals and never implement a plan to accomplish them. A goal without a plan is just a wish.

The Importance of Goals

With the help of this book, you're now able to envision a life of prosperity. Your present task is to breakdown the goal of achieving prosperity into measurable goals. This is important for four reasons:

1. *A vague idea that you're one day going to achieve prosperity is impractical.* Prosperity does not happen by luck or accident. You must determine what it is you want and implement a plan to achieve it.

2. *The journey is long.* As Lao Tzu said, "A journey of a thousand miles begins with a single step." A very large goal, such as prosperity, may seem intimidating. You may feel it's just too overwhelming, like a mountain too steep to climb. When the task seems overwhelming, it's easy to give up and make excuses as to why it was impossible. The Prosperity Track is based on the premise you are in control of your life,

and by taking action, you will slowly but surely make progress along the road of prosperity.

3. ***We all need victories.*** When we succeed at a task we feel good, and our victory encourages us to aim a little higher next time. It's much better to define and tackle ten small challenges, rather than attempt one big challenge. If we try to overcome one big challenge, it's more difficult and the psychological price is much greater if we fail. If we fail at the first small task, it's not a big problem; we can just try again until we succeed. We often avoid tasks too big in scope because they appear impossible.

4. ***By reaching a series of small goals, we can see and measure our progress.*** Imagine you are on a ship that's crossing a vast body of water. In every direction, all you see is water. Day after day, the ship seems to be going forward, but how do you know? Are you making significant progress or are you being blown off course? There are no markers to tell you how you're doing. In contrast, the long road of prosperity has many markers to tell you how far you've come and how far you have to go. You can measure your progress and decide if you need to speed up, slow down, or change direction. There's satisfaction in seeing the markers fall behind you, eventually disappearing in the distance. Seeing your progress gives you the inspiration and incentive to push ahead.

By creating a list of your goals, you can determine which are most important and focus your energy on those. Goal lists should be viewed and updated regularly. By continually viewing your goals, you are more likely to stay on track mentally. Goals change over time. What was important to you five years ago may not be of much importance today. Some people choose to keep their goals on them at all times, while others put them where they will see them every day.

Contrast the stories of Jennifer and Mario. Both struggled with their finances and felt as if they couldn't get ahead despite the fact they both had good jobs. These two perfectly intelligent and deserving people were not yet on the Prosperity Track—they were both stuck at the starting line.

Jennifer knew she wanted a life of prosperity. She envisioned what the foundation looked like, and even had a firm grasp of where she was. She decided to take an unbiased look at her finances and reassess what she was doing with her money. Like many others, she had too much credit card debt and wasn't saving or investing any of her paycheck. This bothered her. She needed to get on the Prosperity Track and lead a happy, stress-free life.

Mario also knew he wanted a life of prosperity. Like Jennifer, he knew what the foundation of prosperity looked like and he knew where he was. He too was able to honestly evaluate his finances. He was a spender, buying stuff he didn't really need—toys like a snowmobile and the latest widescreen 3-D TV—and didn't always pay his bills on time. Consequently, he paid a lot in interest and late fees. His credit rating was damaged due to late payments and his high debt level.

They each responded to their individual challenge differently. Despite being very close to the road of prosperity, Jennifer experienced difficulties getting organized. The task seemed too big and daunting. She thought she had to remake her life in one fell swoop, and that nothing less than a dramatic makeover would solve her problems. For several years, she hemmed and hawed, and continued the same un-prosperous behavior, slowly slipping deeper into debt. Like a ship on a vast trackless sea, she kept sailing… and sailing. Meanwhile her ship was taking on water and slowly sinking. Rather than sailing ahead, she spent most of her time bailing water.

Mario, on the other hand, approached his challenge methodically. He took a hard look at his current situation and set some clear and attainable goals for himself. Individually, the goals weren't huge, but collectively they could have a major impact. They were manageable and could be attained, if not immediately, then within a matter of weeks. When Mario reached his first mini-goal, he felt great personal satisfaction. He felt himself move from the starting line to the actual Prosperity Track. As he passed each marker on the track his confidence grew, and he felt more secure and less stressed. His journey of prosperity had begun with one-step, and then another, and another until he could no longer see where he started.

Make Detailed Goals

Now that we can agree on the importance of setting goals, let's examine the best way to set meaningful goals. Goals must be detailed in order to determine their significance and importance. By answering a few questions, you will be able to determine whether a goal demands commitment and should be prioritized. When setting goals, answer the following questions:

What is the goal? It is important to know exactly what the goal is. Some goals are specific and others are general. The goal "to be healthy" is general compared to the goal of "I want to lose twenty pounds." Getting to the root of the goal will help you set a plan for accomplishing it. Make sure that the goal supports your vision of prosperity.

Why is the goal important? By deeply contemplating the importance of a goal, you are more likely to determine its true significance. "Running a marathon" is an impressive goal, but if you don't like to run, it may not be important to you. Set goals that mean something to you personally, not what might be impressive to others. The goal must be consistent with your vision of prosperity.

When will you complete this goal? Some goals are ongoing, while others have a distinct endpoint. Timeframe can be very motivational for making goals a priority. Be careful not to set unrealistic timeframes. If you do, you may be more likely to keep postponing. Set a plan that includes many small milestones, otherwise you may be tempted to forgo regular progress and opt to make unrealistic results just prior to your deadline. Lasting results come from behavior modification over many months, not quick fixes.

How will you do it? Make a plan to accomplish the goal. The more detailed the better. Write down supportive behaviors you will include and the detracting behaviors you will exclude. Goals without plans are meaningless. If a goal has meaning, make a plan and get it done!

How will you know when you have achieved your goal? Some goals have an end and others are ongoing. Before beginning any plan, make sure you know how you will determine success. Once you begin, it's natural to continue extending your goals. Sometimes goals that continually get extended can negatively affect other goals. If you goal is to be "successful" you may continue pushing long after you have reached an appropriate level of success. By continually increasing your effort, you may detract from other aspects of your life, such as health or relationships. Know when you have achieved enough to support your vision of prosperity.

Make Your Goals Personal

Some people set goals because they want to will impress others. If their neighbor drives a BMW, then they want to drive a Mercedes. If their office mate is a member of an exclusive golf club, then they want to join the club too. If their sibling's kids go to private schools, then they want their kids to go to private schools.

One of the most important principles of the Prosperity Track is the need to focus on *your* values and what *you* envision a prosperous life to be. This doesn't mean you should be a hermit and avoid the company of others, or you shouldn't enjoy life and everything it has to offer. It means you shouldn't be afraid to decide for yourself what's important to you and what's not important.

Jeff was a young executive at a regional bank. He made a good salary, but because he was in the banking industry, he felt enormous pressure to *appear* wealthy and successful. So he leased a high-end Mercedes, and bought expensive suits and a Rolex. Surprisingly, these expensive wares didn't make him feel any happier. He figured this feeling was only temporary and he yearned for the day he would feel happy and successful.

His life changed when he met Shonda. She had a passion for travel and vacationed in exotic places. Jeff realized his pursuit of peer acceptance had suppressed his real interest, which was—you guessed it—travel.

After they were married, Jeff and Shonda decided to rearrange their finances and concentrate on what really interested them. Jeff worked in the world of finance, where image is important. He needed to dress appropriately, but he didn't need a closet filled with custom tailored suits. Instead of trying to compete with their flashier neighbors, he and Shonda bought a modest house, shunned expensive toys, and saved a good portion of their paychecks. When the time came for their first vacation together, they decided to go mountain climbing in Nepal. It was an exciting trip and they made many wonderful memories. Their vision of prosperity included a trip somewhere new every year. To his surprise, many of Jeff's coworkers and bank customers were intrigued by his world travels and exciting tales. By following his passion, he actually gained more prestige, because he wasn't doing the same things everyone else was doing. Shonda and Jeff's passion for travel seemed glamorous and exciting to others. To his surprise, he was envied by many of the very same people he had once tried to impress.

Your goals must be relevant to improving *your* life. Each of us has different guiding values that help us make decisions every day. By focusing on goals that will significantly improve our lives, we can eliminate goals that are just nice to have or that we feel compelled to have. Your goals must mean something to you. A million dollar bank account may sound like the perfect goal to some, but it's ultimately irrelevant. If you're only looking for the prestige of being called a millionaire, a million dollars will never be enough. People who strive solely for monetary rewards will never be satisfied, regardless of the wealth they accumulate. If money and fame are all that you seek, there may be something else going on that you may need to deal with.

Rather than setting an arbitrary monetary target as a goal, I recommend working backwards and begin by determining what would make your life feel more complete. Once you know what you want to improve you can figure out the right goals and the best approach to get you there. Jeff and Shonda worked backwards. Their definition of prosperity included the ability to travel together to interesting places. They identified where they wanted to go and figured out how much it would cost to get there. Once they knew that, they made financial choices that supported their vision of prosperity.

To them, exciting and exotic travel was more gratifying than a big home or an expensive luxury vehicle.

Personal Goal Types

Setting and accomplishing goals is essential to the Prosperity Track. By continually working toward something important to you, you feel energized, enabled, and empowered. By understanding the different types of goals, you can better consider and select goals for each category. There are three main categories of personal goals: internal, external, and relationship. Most people experience the greatest satisfaction when they have goals in each of the three categories.

Internal – Internal goals are typically intangible and include things such as feelings, skills, behavior, knowledge, etc. These goals are unique, because they do not require the involvement or recognition of anyone else. No one has to know whether you have set or achieved an internal goal. For this reason, these goals are the most personal. Because of their unique nature, you may find it difficult to know when you have accomplished an internal goal. Consider setting milestones for skills-based internal goals. Examples of internal goals are:

- Graduating college.
- Becoming more self-confident.
- Learning a new language.
- Becoming vegan.

External – External goals typically involve tangible items or action. This may include a definitive action or a material outcome. Some people receive personal satisfaction for simply accomplishing a goal, while others receive satisfaction by receiving recognition from others. This category of goals tend to be more concrete or absolute. Because of their characteristics, external goals can be defined as complete or incomplete easier than internal goals. Examples of external goals are:

- Losing weight.
- Buying a home.
- Volunteering.
- Visiting Italy.

Relationship – Relationship goals involve others and are ongoing. Prosperous individuals find strong relationships to be important and fulfilling. Relationships are a "two way street" and take work and effort. You are limited to the number of relationships you can maintain. Pursue the relationships that most support your vision of prosperity. Many people consider their relationships to be their most prized possessions. Due to their long-term nature, relationships take the most effort and support. Examples of relationship goals:

- Family.
- Friendship.
- Community.
- Faith.

What's Holding You Back?

We all face a variety of challenges before reaching our goals. When we look from the outside in, some people may appear to have an easier road ahead. But you can never truly appreciate what someone else is going through, unless you see things from their exact point of view. Regardless of the state you are in now, the fact remains you can reach prosperity. By determining what obstacles you face, you can prepare a plan to overcome them. By listing reasons and excuses, you can formulate a plan to conquer each. Although there are plenty of challenges keeping you off the Prosperity Track, none of them are insurmountable.

A difficult truth is that your vision of prosperity may clash with the reality of your immediate environment. Janet was a high school girl who dreamed of becoming a movie star. She wanted to live in a seaside villa, appear in Hollywood films, and be respected for her abilities as an actress. It's very difficult under the best of conditions to become a successful actress. But to make it in show business, you need to have access to opportunities and work tirelessly honing your skills.

Janet's challenge was that she lived on a farm in a small Midwestern town. Now there is nothing wrong with living in a small town in the Midwest, but if you want to act in films, living more than a thousand miles from a center of moviemaking limits your opportunities. There are countless boys and girls, men and women, who imagine a rewarding career in show business and yet do nothing about it. They dream but take no action. They look at the barrier and say, "It's too difficult." They feel they don't have the right looks, the right agent, or the right background. And so they give up.

The annals of Hollywood history are full of examples of people who came from unlikely places, and through tenacity and focus became very prosperous. The actor and comedian Jim Carrey is an excellent example of this. Born in 1962 in Newmarket, Ontario, Canada, Jim was a teenager when his father lost his job, and the family went from being lower middle class to being rock-bottom poor. The family lived out of a van, and at age fifteen Jim quit school to begin working as a janitor to help support his family. Eventually the family moved to Scarborough, Ontario, but Jim never finished high school because he worked full-time to help his family survive and to care for his mother who was battling a severe, chronic illness. He lived in Burlington, Ontario, for eight years, and sporadically attended high school. At that time, Jim's greatest ambition was to land a job at the local Dofasco Steel Mill.

But through it all Jim knew he wanted to be in show business. His dad helped Jim put together a comedy routine of celebrity impersonations, and drove his son to Toronto so he could try his act at the Yuk Yuk comedy club. His first appearances were disasters, but despite the family's persistent poverty, Jim persevered and eventually became a successful nightclub performer. That was his first goal and he achieved it. He made his way to Las Vegas and then onto Hollywood, where he scored small parts in movies and TV shows. Another goal achieved. Finally in 1994, he became an international star with the release of his first major movie lead role as *Ace Ventura:*

Pet Detective. He was thirty-two years old and it had been a long hard road. Certainly there were times of intense discouragement and disappointment, but Jim maintained his priorities and didn't allow himself to get sidetracked.

If you were in Janet's position—or Jim Carrey's for that matter—would you accept the obstacles and give up? Or would you align your circumstances with your goals and forge ahead?

Motivation

Jim Carrey was highly motivated to succeed, as are many prosperous people. Regardless of where we are in life, we all need motivation. However, motivation is not one-size-fits all. We are all individuals who are motivated in different ways.

Find the motivation that leads to success for you. If you're searching for praise and recognition, make sure you share your victories with other people and urge them to do the same. If you're driven by simply doing your best, make sure you do it regularly. When needed, don't be afraid to seek help and counsel from others during your journey.

On his Prosperity Track, Jim Carrey had two powerful motivators. One was his undeniable talent, which he was convinced would lead him to a better life. The other was his first-hand experience with poverty, which motivated him to get on the Prosperity Track and stay there.

Small victories can be big motivation. Every time you reach a milestone you set for yourself, you will feel genuine satisfaction, and it will help you tackle the next milestone.

Earlier in the book, I discussed lottery winners, and the fact that a disappointing majority of big lottery winners suffer reverse motivation after they win. Instead of earning their prosperity through a series of small victories, they are handed a huge "victory" with no sacrifice on their part. They're suddenly rich, but they're unprepared to be prosperous. They have no frame of reference or set of milestones. As a result, too many lottery winners squander their wealth within a few years and end up worse off than they started. Maintaining a high level of wealth is not as easy as it may appear. If lottery winners were to establish a vision of prosperity, and implement a plan for achieving it, they would likely be much better off.

That's why it's so very important to take it one step at a time. Set a series of small goals, and celebrate your progress along the road of prosperity. Prosperity is about achieving a sense of wellbeing. As you achieve goals and live the life you want, make sure you celebrate with the ones you love.

Flash Cards

Remember when you were in grade school and you used flash cards to learn basic things like spelling and the multiplication tables? I'd like to reintroduce you to flash cards. This time we're going to use them to help you along your personal Prosperity Track. We'll also use them to uncover things like fears and obstacles.

Ready? Let's make a set of flash cards. You'll see that each flash card will have two sides. On the front, you'll write the topic, so to speak, and on the back, you'll write the actions needed to fulfill the stated goal or remove the obstacle. Here are some useful categories of flash cards:

Fears – What are you afraid of? We are all fearful at times. Write down your fears on one side and what you can do to overcome that fear on the other side. It may include several steps, gradually gaining confidence and result in overcoming your fear. Having a plan helps build courage. Think creatively. Ask friends and family for ideas and support.

Obstacles – Write down your obstacles on one side and how you can overcome them on the back. Have a proactive plan for tackling your obstacles. Focus on implementing positive changes in behavior.

Mental blocks – Many of us have mental blocks that interfere with our ability to reach our goals. The more we challenge our own perception the more we can achieve. Ask people how they view you and what they think your greatest skills are. You will be shocked what they tell you. If someone tells you something nice, write it down and refer to it later. Sometimes we all need a confidence boost. You have the ability to achieve the life you desire, but it will take having confidence in yourself. Although unfortunate at times, our brains are rich with creativity and imagination. We often imagine things that are untrue and unrelated to us. Sometimes you will need to take a moment to relax and get out of your own head.

Guiding values – We all have values that guide us through the many decisions we face every day. Write down your top twenty values (view list at www.prosperitytrack.com/tools) that define who you are and what you stand for. From there you can refine the list further and select your top ten. By continuously narrowing down your guiding values, you can better define what makes you happy and creates fulfillment. When you understand your guiding values, you can reenergize and aim directly at making yourself happy. On the back of each flash card, write down the activities you do or need to do to maintain this guiding value. If family is your most important value, but you choose to spend time with friends rather than your family, you must determine whether family truly is a guiding value. Be honest with yourself and choose the values that truthfully guide your decisions.

Your Fifty Personal Goals

After completing the exercises above, you are ready to begin creating your ideal prosperous life. You will better understand who you are, what you want, and what makes you happy.

Next, I want you to list fifty things you want to accomplish. Whether it's cleaning the garage or learning to speak French, you should write it down. It's easy to get started, but most people stall around twenty-five. Push through and keep going. No matter how trivial a goal may seem, write it down. Most of us take several days to get to fifty. Carry the list with you and write things down as you go about your day. This may even become sort of a "bucket list." The goals should be yours and worth achieving in your mind.

Prioritize Your Goals

Fifty may seem like a big number, but remember you're including all sorts of goals, big and small. We have only a limited supply of time and money, and we may not be able to achieve every one of our goals simultaneously. You must prioritize the goals that are most important and have the greatest impact. Focus your efforts on the goals that mean the most to you. You should commit time and effort to make regular progress on your highest priority goals.

Although some goals may take a lifetime to accomplish, others can be completed in short order. You should be working on a combination of short-term and long-term goals at all times. We all need little victories in life and it's important to write down things we want to do and get them done. Small successes lead to big successes over time. You have to keep dreaming big. Once you know how to make positive changes, you will be tempted to try bigger goals. Working diligently toward something is one of the most fulfilling activities you can do. After accomplishing a long-term goal, many people feel a little lost. They committed so much time and effort to accomplish the goal, they miss it once it's gone.

Tim and Maria were a happily married couple who wanted to become not just comfortable, but prosperous. They wanted to maximize their resources and focus on achieving a set of goals that meant something special to them. So they made their list of fifty goals. I won't list them all, but here are a few:

1. Remodel the bathroom.

3. Visit Tim's mother more often.

6. Enroll in an evening class for computer graphics. (Tim)

12. Spend two weeks in the Bahamas.

13. Get Tim a new suit for the holiday party.

19. Clean out the garage.

21. Fund 401(k) accounts to the maximum.

23. Weed the flowerbed by the kitchen door.

26. Clean the inside of the car.

31. Pay off all the credit cards.

34. If possible, refinance the mortgage at a lower rate.

38. Practice the piano. (Maria)

42. Go to a Jimmy Buffet concert.

47. Write more blog posts. (Maria)

48. Lose ten pounds. (Tim)

50. Read the new best-selling thriller everyone is talking about.

As you can see, the list ranges from easy to challenging. After they made this long random list, Tim and Maria grouped the entries under the following four categories:

A. Short-term and easy. (Clean the inside of the car.)

B. Short-term and challenging. (Investigate a mortgage refinance.)

C. Long-term and easy. (Visit Tim's mother more often.)

D. Long-term and challenging. (Pay off all the credit cards.)

The degree of satisfaction varies for each category, with small satisfaction for category A and the highest satisfaction for category D.

In addition, they grouped their goals according to which ones would promote their journey to prosperity. Cleaning the inside of the car is a nice short-term goal, but it's not particularly relevant to Tim and Maria's overall prosperity. However, things like paying off the credit cards and spending two weeks in the Bahamas directly impact their sense of prosperity.

Tim and Maria agreed to take action on each of the four categories of goals each week. Not a week would go by without positive action being taken. For example—to use the goals mentioned earlier—it was pretty easy for Tim to clean the inside of the car, he just had to dedicate an hour to the task. One goal checked off! Meanwhile, Maria contacted a mortgage provider and completed a preliminary application for a refinance. Another goal checked off, or at least in progress. Visiting Tim's mother was not difficult, but required planning ahead. Regular visits made his mother very happy. The last goal, paying off credit card debt, obviously would take a long time. Tim and Maria sat down together and listed their credit cards by the amounts owed and the corresponding interest rates. They had three credit cards. One card carried a noticeably higher interest rate, so the balance on that card was the most expensive. (Remember, a credit card is nothing more than an expensive credit line.) They decided to make substantial extra payments to that card so it would be paid off in six months. Once the card with the highest interest rate was paid off, they would then shift the previous monthly payment amount to the card with the next highest interest rate. When that one was paid off, they'd shift all of their previous payment amounts to the last remaining card.

If you want to stay on the Prosperity Track, do what Tim and Maria did and take your list of fifty goals and sort them by priority. You may find, for example, that fixing a leak in the roof is a much higher priority than going to the opera (although I know some people who would rather go to the opera than fix their roof; everyone has their own priorities!). After you select your top goals, determine a game plan for achieving each one. Some of your goals will be simple and easy to attain, while others will be complex and take more time and effort. It's amazing the satisfaction you can gain from accomplishing nagging goals. Sometimes there is something you have always wanted to do, but you never made it a priority. Whether it's a friend you've been meaning to call or a restaurant you've been dying to try, write it down and then do it. After you do, you will feel a sense of accomplishment and more importantly, it will no longer be an irritating distraction. Rather than set goals once a year, keep a running list of goals. As goals are accomplished or changed, update your list.

There may be obstacles, too. If you prepare in advance for obstacles, you will be in a better position to triumph later on.

A good example of someone overcoming obstacles is the singer Tony Bennett. A superstar in the nineteen-fifties and sixties, but as the seventies ended, Bennett found himself with no recording contract, no manager, and was working in much smaller venues. He had developed a drug addiction and the Internal Revenue Service was trying to seize his Los Angeles home. He was destined to become just another washed-up showbiz relic, miles away from the road of prosperity.

His son Danny Bennett assumed the role of his father's manager. Danny moved his father back to New York, got his father's expenses under control, and began booking him in colleges and small theaters. By 1986, Tony Bennett was once again signed to Columbia Records.

But that was merely the beginning. Danny suspected that while his father's traditional audience was fading, younger audiences, unfamiliar with Tony Bennett, would respond favorably to his music if given the opportunity. The very qualities that made Tony Bennett seem square and old-fashioned could, with the right approach, be made to seem cool again. Danny was able to arrange his father appearances on *Late Night with David Letterman, Late Night with Conan O'Brien, The Simpsons,* and various other programs catering to younger viewers. He was even invited to perform at a series of benefit concerts orchestrated by alternative rock radio stations.

Together, Danny and Tony Bennett had confronted a huge obstacle—Tony's career nosedive —and, through a series of attainable goals, put him firmly back on the Prosperity Track.

Previous Goals

We all have set goals and resolutions in the past. Did you accomplish all of yours? I surely didn't accomplish all of mine. By asking tough questions of yourself, you can better understand why you didn't achieve your goals. This will take an honest, hard look in the mirror, but the outcome will be powerful. Look deep inside and determine whether you truly gave it all that you had.

Why did you give up or abandon the goal? – People fail for many reasons. Some goals require more effort or time than the person is willing to give. While others do not have the resources to follow through to the end. We often give up on ourselves when the going gets tough. Though it's easier to quit in the short-term, regret can be painful and tends last a long time. Could you have given it more effort? What could you have done differently to change the outcome?

Why was the goal important? – Most of us set tangible goals, such as a big house or nice car. But many intangible goals, such as improved health or more meaningful relationships, are better at improving wellbeing. If a goal is important, then it must command time and resources. Although setbacks occur, if you are committed, failure is an unlikely outcome. Goals must be important to you. Trying to achieve something that will impress others is usually counterproductive. Accomplish things that will make you and your family happier and feeling prosperous.

Let's return to Janet, the aspiring actress who lived on a farm in the Midwest. In high school, she acted in school plays, but after graduation, she didn't know how to proceed. Moving to New York or Los Angeles seemed like a huge risk and she had very few resources. So she put her goal aside and got a job in a restaurant in the small town where she lived. That was how she lived her life, with a huge unresolved goal stuck in her head.

Two years after she graduated from high school and had gone to work at the restaurant, a Hollywood production company announced they were making a movie nearby and needed extras. The film was to be set on a farm and the company desired authentic farm folks for small parts. Luckily, Janet had taken several acting classes at her local community college and was a regular performer at improv shows. She auditioned using what she had learned in class and on stage, and was awarded a part.

The experience was fun, but something else would change Janet's life forever. The casting director told her she had good screen presence and she should consider auditioning for more parts. But to do this Janet had to go to Los Angeles. After much soul-searching, she decided to use her savings to travel to Los Angeles and live for a year. If after one year she had gotten nowhere, she would have no choice but to return home.

Now, Janet had a new goal: survive for one year as an aspiring actress in Hollywood. This goal seemed manageable; if she couldn't make it work, she could always come home. Although the work was hard and unpredictable, she was committed. Despite the constant hustle and rejection of the acting business, she did feel some personal satisfaction. The satisfaction of achieving her dream far outweighed the possible embarrassment of failing and returning home.

In Hollywood, Janet got the parts you'd expect for an unknown: low-budget TV commercials and extra work in films. But Janet got a job as a waitress and put herself on a tight budget, and when the year was up, she was able to stay in Los Angeles. Her new goal was to get a speaking part—even a very small one—in a film or TV show. At this point in her new career, this goal seemed attainable. A year earlier—when she was still working at the restaurant in her hometown—this goal would have seemed far-fetched.

Over the years, Janet continued working in restaurants and made slow and steady progress in her acting career. She never got to be a superstar and was never a leading lady, but she worked steadily and saved her money. She bought a little bungalow in the Hollywood Hills and worked with a well-known improv group. The most important thing is that Janet felt prosperous. She was on the Prosperity Track and loving every minute of it. After putting her goal to become an actress on the back burner, an unexpected opportunity gave her the confidence she needed to set realistic goals for herself and achieve her dreams. Although Janet didn't have a big bank account or fancy car, she did what she loved every day. In her mind, she felt like she was living large! Remember, prosperity isn't a number. It's how you feel about your life that matters.

Chapter Four Takeaways

As you have seen, setting goals is an important part of achieving prosperity. By creating a list of goals important to you, you are able to focus your efforts and not waste time or energy. Positive motivation will energize and empower you to tackle small goals that collectively have a major impact. No goal is too small or inconsequential. When unaccomplished, even small goals can detract from your enjoyment of life. Write down and do the things you have always wanted to. Take steps every day to get you closer to your prosperous lifestyle. If you don't know where you want to go, how will you know if you get there?

Prosperity in Practice

What is your motivation for making a change?

If you have tried before, what is different this time?

What are you committed to doing?

How can you improve your prosperity?

Prosperity in Action

Keep a record of current goals and completed goals. It's nice to have something you are striving for, but it's also important to remember achievements.

Make a list of fifty goals. Assign a difficulty level and expected duration. Implement a strategy for recognizing completion. It is not always easy to know if a goal has been completed, formulate milestones to help you determine completion.

Create and review your flash cards. Having a visual reminder of your goals will help keep you on track.

Chapter Five

Prosperity by Design

> *"Efforts and courage are not enough without purpose and direction."*
>
> **John F. Kennedy**

As we learned in the previous sections, prosperity does not happen by accident; prosperity is intentional. Breaking down your vision of prosperity into smaller attainable goals is important, but directed action makes them happen. What we do is far more important than what we write or say. Act in a way that best represents your guiding values and your vision of prosperity. Be proactive. If your habits and lifestyle support your vision of prosperity, keep them going. If there are goals and aspirations you have yet to attempt, make it a point to try. Review your current situation and see where you want to make changes.

Recall, our definition of prosperity is:

The personal state of achievement, contentment, and wellbeing.

Prosperity encompasses many fundamentals of your lifestyle, including: health, wealth, happiness, relationships, community, etc. The three main components needed to achieve prosperity are: time, money, and effort. Accomplishing your goals will require one, two, or all three of these components. Your resources and preferences will determine the most appropriate combination needed to achieve your goals. Depending on your current situation and vision of prosperity you may need to assess which components and what behaviors are most beneficial.

Self-Talk

Each of us has an inner monologue or inner voice that speaks to us throughout the day. This is the little voice that tells us "don't forget to pick up the dry cleaning" or "I really should go to the gym today." Most of the time, this voice is positive and guides us sensibly. However, sometimes this voice is uncooperative and possibly negative. Negative self-talk can be the manifestation of inner feelings and insecurities. It's common to feel scared, nervous, or insecure. Unfortunately, negative self-talk converts these feelings into a negative conversation repeatedly playing in your head. Negative self-talk can be emotionally and physically draining. When we engage in negative self-talk, we think "I don't want to go the gym, because people will laugh at me" or "I'm not what they are looking for so why bother applying." In reality, the negative thoughts we think are just that, our thoughts. Most of the time, we are the only one who has this negative opinion.

If there is a consistent theme to your inner dialogue, consider challenging your thought process and test the notion. If you think someone doesn't like you, ask them (politely of course). What's the worst that can happen, they like you less? It is better to confront your negative thoughts than to continue their destructive nature unopposed. As an alternative, you may be able to overcome your negative inner thoughts by engaging in positive self-talk.

If you find yourself having negative thoughts, create a series of positive affirmations that you review daily. Begin each day by repeating your personal affirmations out loud. Carry them with you. Memorize them. If you find yourself needing some positive motivation, close your eyes, take a deep breath, and repeat your affirmations. Here are some sample positive affirmations:

- I am strong and my actions are powerful.
- I live each day with purpose and direction.
- I give love and respect, and deserve the same in return.
- I am my own person and I live as I feel I should.
- I will love, learn, and laugh each and every day.
- I am stronger today than I was yesterday and I will be even stronger tomorrow.

Actions manifest from thinking. Create a set of positive affirmations reflective of the person you are and the person you want to be. Write them down. Carry them with you until you commit them to memory. Say them when you need a confidence boost or you feel insecure. Positive self-talk will help you conquer negative thinking, and will empower you operate at your highest potential.

Interest vs. Commitment

There is an important distinction between being interested and being committed. Each of us is interested in a wide variety of things, but we are committed to very few. To be interested is to give special attention to something, while commitment involves doing something regardless of opposition. Interests come and go, but commitments last much longer. Although you should have both in your life, serious matters deserve your commitment. Interest is great for hobbies, but may not be appropriate for relationships. With limited hours in the day, we can only be committed to a finite number of people, activities, and organizations.

Most of us can muster only a limited amount of additional effort and therefore must prioritize our commitments. Commit yourself to activities closely related to your guiding values. If those values truly guide your actions, dedicate as much time and effort to the values that mean the most to you. You can be interested in many things, but be careful not to spread yourself too thin. Having too many interests may deter you from what you consider most important. Life is too short to remain unhappy or conflicted.

Tony and Nikki Berti co-founded the Las Vegas-based Goodie Two Shoes Foundation. Their organization's mission is to provide disadvantaged children and children in crisis with new shoes and socks, as well as other items deemed essential for good health and positive development. Tony and Nikki modeled their first event after a similar event they volunteered for during Tony's playing days with the NFL's San Diego Chargers. In coordination with *Make a Difference Day 2003*, they gave away 227 pairs of shoes. Although they felt the event was a success, they wanted to expand their efforts and help more children. Throughout the years, their efforts grew consistently, distributing 512 pairs of shoes in 2004, 1024 in 2005, 1256 in 2006, 1496 in 2007, and 3465 in 2008!

Following their immensely successful 2008 giveaway, Tony and Nikki realized they had exceeded their capacity to volunteer. Their charitable work required so much effort and attention, it detracted from their family and work. They could not continue to operate their charity this way without compromising other important aspects of their lives. If Goodie Two Shoes was to continue its mission, it needed to change. Tony and Nikki faced the tough decision of either reducing the size of their annual event or taking Goodie Two Shoes to the next level. But, if they were going to expand the organization and outfit more children, they needed to raise money.

Now committed to the goal of expanding their charity, Nikki aggressively applied for grants. She was dedicated to making the organization bigger and better, helping even more disadvantaged children in the process. With the help of a sizeable grant in 2009, Goodie Two Shoes began mobile outreach in addition to their annual giveaway. Their foundation grew so vastly that it demanded full-time commitments from both Nikki and Tony. What originally began as an interest now required their full commitment.

It took Goodie Two Shoes seven years to cumulatively distribute 10,000 pairs of shoes. Now the foundation provides more than 10,000 pairs of shoes, socks, and essential items to underprivileged children each year. Tony and Nikki now work for the foundation full-time and conduct two major fundraising events and twenty-five shoe distributions a year. The Bertis are a prime example of doing well by doing good. Their vision of prosperity includes raising their sons Brennan and Easton, but also helping disadvantaged children throughout Southern Nevada. You can learn more about the Goodie Two Shoes Foundation by visiting www.goodietwoshoes.org.

Now is the time to commit and achieve what you have always desired. The path may be rocky and challenging, but anything worth achieving is never easy. Be strong and fight on! You deserve it.

Prioritizing

Each of us has limited time and resources, so we must allocate them in the most effective manner. Prioritize where your time and money are spent. If left solely to chance, you will often choose incorrectly. Don't let what you want right now get in the way of what you really want. Prioritize where you spend your time and money. Go back to your top ten guiding values. You know your ten most important motivators, but have you aligned your resources to pursue these values?

I have met many people who tell me their top guiding value is family. When I inquire about their relationship with their family, I am surprised to learn they don't spend time with or communicating with other family members. They tell me about the gifts or money they send, but not about being present in the relationship. And they are surprised when they don't have a great relationship with their family. Sending a check is not enough. Guiding values demand you exert great effort in their direction. You have to prioritize your time and make a difference.

Some people have a difficult time prioritizing their spending. A great exercise is to review your monthly expenses and rank them from the most important to the least important. Although you feel something is important, when you compare it to other expenditures, it may not be as important as you previously thought. This exercise is crucial for people who spend more than they earn each month. Begin with your monthly income and subtract each expenditure as you move down the list, once you run out of money, *stop*! Anything left to spend after your money runs out is the lowest priority and unfortunately must be eliminated. You should notice the elimination of things that are "wants" and not "needs." For people who continually overspend, this exercise can be painful. Their spending is out of control, despite believing they have complete control of their behavior. If your goal is to save a certain amount of money each month, begin with that amount and then proceed to your other expenses. Visit www.prosperitytrack.com/tools for a worksheet to help you prioritize spending.

Budgeting

Budgeting is a fundamental activity necessary for prosperity. Simply stated, budgeting means mastering your expenses within the confines of your income. In Chapter Three, I introduced you to the *Budget Timeline* and *Budget Worksheet*. As part of your *Prosperity Plan*, I want you to proactively examine your income and spending before each month. At the end of each month, look again and see what happened. Based on the results, set specific goals designed to enhance your sense of prosperity. Make your goals specific.

As a general rule, I recommend that you spend ten percent less than you earn. How you allocate your spending is up to you, because it will depend upon your personal goals. While many goals are directly related to money, others are not. For example, unless your mother lives in another city and there are significant travel costs involved, visiting her may not require financial sacrifice. On the other hand, if your definition of prosperity is to own a lakefront cottage with a private dock, then you'll have to set sizable financial goals, and you may have to cut back on expenses in other areas.

Unless you enjoy accounting, budgeting may be a tedious task you avoid. Fortunately, there are a wide variety of digital and online tools that can make budgeting easy even for beginners.

If you have a checking account—which I assume you do—make sure you have a debit card. These cards are terrific because your bank probably offers online banking that tracks debit card purchases as you make them. In the past, if you wrote a paper check at the grocery store, you would have to wait until you received your month-end statement to see if it was cashed. If you had trouble remembering to balance your checkbook, it was easy to end up with a bounced check and an expensive overdraft fee.

William was one of those people who just couldn't be bothered to balance his checkbook. He made a good salary, but money just seemed to flow in and out of his account, occasionally leaving him short at the end of the month. Then he signed up for online banking and got a debit card, which he used for practically everything. He would routinely log on and instantly have access to his current balance and all recent transactions. Now, he knew exactly what his balance was. He later signed up for automatic payments for his utilities, forever avoiding late fees.

Some debit and credit cards will even report your charges by category. When you open your statement, either online or paper, you see the various categories such as restaurants, travel, or retail stores, along with the purchases in each category. It's a convenient way to see at a glance where your money is going. Take advantage of these new budgeting tools. They can help even the most mathematically challenged person control his or her cash flow.

For the more sophisticated household budget manager, consider one of the many software solutions designed for home budgeting. The most popular software brand is Quicken, with products ranging from a relatively simple program that tracks your account activity to versions that help you with your home business, investments, and taxes.

Only by regularly reviewing your financial transactions, will you notice patterns of spending. Initially, you should try to budget weekly and set limits for unbudgeted expenditures. Most of us know when we are going to have expenditures and the approximate amounts. By determining what you expect to spend at the beginning of the week, you are in a better position to work within those confines. By anchoring on a certain level of spending, you're more likely to avoid impulsive and wasteful spending. In the early phase, budgeting should be done at the beginning and end of each week. Once you have mastered the process you can move to budgeting monthly. It is crucial to have an understanding of what comes in and goes out of your bank accounts. If you routinely overspend, drastic actions must be taken, such as cutting up your credit cards, eliminating certain activities, and even distancing yourself from friends or family members who are bad influences. Beware of things, activities or people that will derail your prosperity. It's true that misery loves company, so beware of how you spend your time. Surround yourself with people and activities that are uplifting and joyous.

Employment and Entrepreneurship

Prosperity results in being able to do what you want, when you want to do it. For one person it may mean being able to vacation in the Bahamas; for someone else it may mean having the time to write a novel. Although expense management is important to prosperity, increasing one's income may also be helpful. For people who do not earn enough money to reach their prosperity potential, there are ways to increase income. In many cases, people who wish to improve themselves financially have skills and talents being ignored. People in this category can utilize their talents to earn income outside of their normal job. A little extra income can go a long way to improving your lifestyle. It will take effort and in some cases time to get moving, but it's definitely an option to help you reach your ideal lifestyle. People who are underemployed need to examine why they work where they do, and try to develop the skills or attitude to reach the next level.

Too many people get comfortable in their current role and fail to find their true calling. Fear of the unknown can be debilitating. It's easy to feel resigned to your fate, and to say, "Well, this is the salary I make, and I can't do any better, so I'll just have to live with it."

Companies are always interested in increasing revenue, decreasing costs, and improving service. If you can add value in these areas, you can always find great opportunities. You must be in a mental and emotional mindset that allows you to succeed. Leaving your comfort zone and trying new things is difficult for many people, and becoming an entrepreneur can seem downright scary. Try something small and gradually work your way up. If you do not want to excel in your current company, look for alternate employment. If you like your job, look to increase your income elsewhere. Start a home based business you can operate at night and on weekends. It's not the easy route, but true prosperity rarely comes easily.

In 2001, a housewife in Grand Haven, Michigan named Kim Lavine noticed that if you stuffed a fabric bag with corn kernels and put the bag in the microwave, the pillow would get wonderfully toasty warm, and the corn held the heat for a long time. Kim started making the microwavable pillows as gifts for her kids' teachers. She assembled them at her kitchen table, and stitched them with a sewing machine she barely knew how to use.

Soon after she began her hobby, her husband lost his job, which motivated her to consider turning her pastime into a source of income.

She went from selling pillows out of her truck to setting up mall kiosks. In 2002, she incorporated her company, Green Daisy. Within two years, Lavine's Wuvit spa therapy pillow was sold in national chains, including Saks Fifth Avenue, Macy's, and Bed Bath & Beyond. By 2006, the pillow was generating more than a million dollars in sales annually.

To expand her business, Lavine introduced a pajama line and then a home décor line. She became a business consultant, and wrote about her success in *Mommy Millionaire: How I Turned My Kitchen Table Idea into a Million Dollars and How You Can, Too*, which was published in 2009.

Not all entrepreneurial businesses are started at kitchen tables. Terry Finley felt like he was stuck in his job selling life insurance and wanted to get on the road of prosperity. Terry knew his *Prosperity Plan* didn't include selling insurance, but he was unsure what other options he had. Terry decided to explore his passion for horseracing. One day in 1991, he bought a horse named Sunbelt for five thousand dollars. After Sunbelt won his first race that year, Finley ran some small ads in racing papers and attracted an investor, who put another five thousand dollars into Sunbelt. Within two months Terry bought his second horse, Cal's Zen Jr., and then continued buying more horses on credit cards. It was a huge risk—as I've mentioned, credit cards are an expensive way to borrow money—but Terry was committed.

That same year he quit his job and founded West Point Thoroughbreds, a Saratoga Springs, New York-based racehorse syndication management company. Today, West Point Thoroughbreds owns eighty syndicated horses and the stable has earned over nineteen million dollars in winnings.

Distinguishing Wants from Needs

It's important you are able to differentiate wants from needs. Needs are necessary for sustaining life and include: food, water, shelter, and clothing. We often trick ourselves into believing we truly need something when we really don't. When looking to improve your life, it's important to separate needs from wants, and allocate resources to achieve your goals. We spend too much time and money on things we don't need or even really want.

It's natural to want nice things as our income grows. When we get a raise or promotion, we are immediately tempted to spend our newly earned money. However, too many people fall into the trap of continuously increasing their monthly expenditures to match each and every increase in income. As mentioned previously, this behavior is referred to as *"lifestyle inflation."* Lifestyle inflation is a real and very dangerous condition. This behavior usually results in a vast array of debt payments each month. More and more income is needed to facilitate an increased level of spending. These expenditures almost always fall in the category of wants. We all need a method of transportation to go to work or the store, but no one truly needs a brand new Rolls Royce Phantom. Depending on your level of wealth, you may be able to purchase a luxury vehicle, but doing so should never jeopardize your future prosperity.

Increase your lifestyle modestly with each raise in pay. Be careful not to set the bar too high too fast. If something drastic were to happen to your new income, would you be able to support your new lifestyle? Once someone has had a "taste" of the good life, it's almost impossible to accept a lower standard of living. It's important to treat yourself, but not cheat yourself.

Evaluate Prices Relative to Your Income

Many people compare prices to how much money they make per hour. If you make $20 an hour at your job, an item costing $100 requires five hours of work to purchase (even more when you consider taxes). For example, Simon was working in his garage one day and accidentally broke his watch. It had been several years since his last watch purchase, and he was considering buying a stylish new watch. Although there were several watches he liked, he was most interested in a blue faced Movado that cost $1,000. Although Simon didn't have the money in his bank account, he could purchase the watch using the 12-month, 0% interest promotion the store was offering. Simon decided to compare the $1,000 watch to his $45,000 a year salary. By dividing his salary by the 2,000 working hours in the year (fifty-two weeks minus two weeks of vacation, times forty hours a week), Simon made about $22.50 an hour. The watch would cost him more than he made in a week working. Although Simon could afford the monthly payment, he felt the watch wasn't worth working over forty-four hours to pay for. He opted to buy a similar looking watch that cost less than $100, equal to less than five hours earnings.

Chapter Five Takeaways

Prosperity is never accidental or a surprise. It takes massive effort and discipline to become truly prosperous. You will have to make tough decisions and prioritize your time as well as your spending. If left to chance, your prosperity will suffer. Before each month, make a budget and do your best to stick to it. If you spend more than you make, consider finding additional or alternate employment. Although most people work for an employer, do not rule out having your own business in addition to your job. Find an activity that you enjoy, do well, and one that someone will pay you to do on nights or weekends. A little extra income can go a long way to feeling prosperous.

Prosperity in Practice

Do you earn enough money to support your vision of prosperity?

Have you prioritized your wants and needs?

Do you create a monthly budget before each month and review it after the month?

Chapter Six

Develop Your Prosperity Plan

We cannot solve our problems with the same thinking we used
when we created them.

Albert Einstein

Congratulations—you've come a long way! You have learned what it
means to be prosperous, and hopefully you have begun developing
your vision of prosperity. I introduced goals and their importance to
your continued prosperity. These lessons and exercises will be
extremely important as you develop your *Prosperity Plan*.
Developing your vision of prosperity will be the most important part
of your *Prosperity Plan*. To help you form the basis for your vision, I
revealed my definition of prosperity:

The personal state of achievement, contentment, and wellbeing.

Your vision of prosperity may involve your family, career, travel, hobbies, or community involvement. Although you need money to pay for things, money alone is not the goal. It's how you use your money that matters.

With this foundation in place, we're now ready to plan your journey on the Prosperity Track. Your *Prosperity Plan* is your road map. It includes the signs and markers that will guide you and ensure you don't wander off course. While your plan is flexible over time, you need to hold yourself accountable. It's ok to make adjustments from time to time, but these adjustments should not deter you from accomplishing your goals. Be consistent with your target lifestyle and continue to make progress, whether big or small.

In the following pages, I will walk you step-by-step through the Prosperity Track planning process. I hope you find the process fun and rewarding. As we discussed in Chapter Four, establishing goals is necessary to better formulate a plan. You must create and implement a plan that will ultimately transform your life.

Your Prosperity Plan

The work you have done thus far will be instrumental in creating your *Prosperity Plan*. The *Prosperity Plan* is a one-page document that contains your vision of prosperity, guiding values, goals, strategy statements, and milestones & rewards. Visit www.prosperitytrack.com/tools for the *Prosperity Plan* template. By developing and implementing your plan, you will be energized, enabled, and empowered to achieve your greatest potential. Let's examine each of the plan's sections:

Vision of Prosperity – By now you have built a vision of prosperity in your mind. Now, it is time to write it down. It may be difficult at first, but define in words what your vision of prosperity looks like and feels like. Include the details that you find most important and rewarding.

Guiding Values – In Chapter Four, you selected your top ten guiding values. These values should be represented in every decision you make. Your guiding values must be consistent with your vision of prosperity. What you value in life determines what you consider a prosperous life to be.

Goals – In Chapter Four you learned about the importance of goals and the different categories of goals. Select and write down goals in each of the three categories. These should be your biggest priority goals. These goals will help dictate your future behavior.

Strategy Statements – Thus far, you have written down what is important to you and what you want to achieve. Now, write down what you will do to achieve it. Your behavior will determine what you can accomplish. Compile a set of things you will do and perhaps not do. For instance, you might write, "I will call my mother every Sunday" or "I will not eat ice cream late at night." Consider behavior that has benefitted you, and behaviors you believe will benefit you in the future. Your *Prosperity Plan* will contain the behaviors that best support your ideal prosperous lifestyle. These statements will guide you along the Prosperity Track.

Milestones & Rewards – All work and no play may be the most efficient track to prosperity, but it's also the most unlikely. You need to treat yourself when you reach a particular milestone. It's easier to restrain yourself when you know a reward is forthcoming. Be mindful that rewards should be appropriate to the milestone and should not derail your prosperity. Rewards, like the accomplishment, should make you feel good and never make you feel regretful.

Most personal trainers recommend a weekly "cheat day" for their clients. Clients who eat a healthy diet six days a week, and then eat whatever they want one day a week, are more likely to have long-term success. We know it's better to eat properly every day, but that's just not practical. By having a reward each week, you are more likely to stick to your fitness program. Long-term prosperity works the same way. Treat yourself, but don't cheat yourself.

Formulating Milestones & Rewards

It would be nice if being on the road of prosperity were enough of its own reward, needing no other tangible inducement. Rebecca, whose personal goal of world travel is essentially one big reward, has no problem staying on the Prosperity Track. For most of us, staying on the Prosperity Track requires some degree of sacrifice, and we're more motivated to stay on track when we experience the benefits of our emerging prosperity. In the interim, we should reward ourselves for our continued success.

Rewards come in many shapes and sizes. Positive feelings are associated with accomplishing goals and there are often tangible benefits as well. The rewards you choose to give yourself must benefit your life and represent your vision of prosperity. If rewards do not fit your prosperous lifestyle, consider a different reward. If the rewards are insignificant compared to the effort and resources required, there may not be enough motivation. Rewards should be proportionate to the effort and dedication required.

You must remember that the reward must never result in a setback to your journey. "Two steps forward and one step back" is not a recipe for success on the Prosperity Track.

With that in mind, let's consider the story of Larry and Monique. As a young couple, they had some big expenditures in their future, including buying a home. Larry was an electrician who made a good middle-class income, while Monique worked as a teacher. Together they hoped to earn enough and save for the down payment on a home. With a combined income of $80,000 per year, they knew they could afford a home costing them no more than 28% of their income, which is the limit set by many mortgage companies. With a monthly income of roughly $6,600, they calculated they could afford to pay about $1,800 a month for a mortgage. But what could $1,800 a month buy? Using a free online mortgage calculator, they calculated they could buy a house for $330,000 with a thirty-year fixed-rate mortgage at the current interest rate of 4.5%. Their goal was to save ten percent of the purchase price for a down payment, which would be $33,000. Their loan amount would be $297,000. Visit www.prosperitytrack.com/tools for various tools and links for mortgage calculation.

Saving $33,000 is very aggressive for any person or couple making $80,000 a year. Fortunately, Larry and Monique had previous savings of $10,000 and received another $5,000 in wedding gifts. Their goal was to save the additional $18,000 within two years. They needed to save $750 each month to achieve their down payment goal.

Meanwhile they still had to pay rent and buy all the usual necessities. After completing a budget, they knew they could achieve their saving goal by reducing some entertainment expenses and living on a tighter budget.

This worked fine for about six months, during which they diligently stashed away $3,300. But over dinner one night, they confessed to each other that they were going crazy! They each felt like their savings plan was causing them to have absolutely no fun in life. It was all work and save, work and save. It was too much of a lifestyle shock, and they didn't feel they could continue saving at that pace.

They addressed their problem in two ways. Their first idea was to research opportunities for having fun that required little to no money. Monique discovered numerous local public parks and beaches. Larry found some museums offering free admission to local residents. They resolved to take advantage of these resources they previously didn't know existed.

The second idea involved spending some money. They decided that for every $1,100 they saved, they would spend $100 on an evening out. It seemed like a reasonable reward, and they agreed to alternate choosing the reward—Monique would choose first, and then Larry, and so on.

Their strategy was successful because it not only broke the monotony of just working to save, but it also provided periodic rewards that allowed them to stay on track. Knowing that each time they deposited $1,100 into their savings account would earn them a reward, made saving much easier. People have an easier time working towards a series of small short-term goals rather than one big long-term goal. Smaller, more frequent goals are still satisfying and the rewards always seem within reach.

Your Personal Journal

Budgeting is not always just about the numbers. Those little digits on the screen represent real things you pay for: new clothes, a birthday gift, that dream vacation, or even life-saving medicines. It's easy for an accountant to say, "You've got to cut your spending by ten percent," but it's difficult to make decisions about things we have an emotional connection to.

Try keeping a journal of your experiences for a few months. Don't just keep track of things that you spent money on, keep track of things you didn't spend money on. If you stay home for your anniversary rather than going out to an expensive restaurant, that is big win! You made a conscious decision to prioritize your long-term prosperity and you should recognize it. Record and celebrate your good decision.

Keep track of how you feel at the time you make decisions. Emotions often cloud our judgment and are important to review when we regain our composure. Your actions and feelings are important, but our thoughts and memories often mislead us. We unknowingly change our perception of the past after learning the outcome. Looking back, you'll appreciate seeing your thoughts and feelings as things were happening. Although this is a personal journal and does not have to be viewed by anyone else, feel free to share your writing with a trusted confidant or partner.

Rachel was proud of her marriage to Leonard—they had a nice house, two cars, and three great kids. But after ten years of marriage they still struggled. It wasn't terrible—they always managed to get by—but it just seemed as though they were never able to feel truly prosperous.

In an effort to see the big picture of their spending, Rachel began keeping a personal journal. She wrote about the things that meant a lot to her and her husband: holidays and birthdays, or when one of the kids did something special in school. Rachel's daily journal entries highlighted the experiences that provided her family the most fulfillment, rather than the most wealth.

After a few months of tracking, Rachel showed her journal to her husband, and they both noticed something interesting: very few of Rachel's entries mentioned the exclusive golf club they had been members of since before the kids were born. Leonard had once fancied playing golf on the weekends, but lately he only played once or twice a year. Rachel took the kids there occasionally, but she recently grew tired of the stuffy atmosphere. After serious contemplation, they realized they didn't get much benefit from the five thousand dollar a year country club. It made more sense to take that five thousand dollars and put it into a Section 529 college fund for the kids. A 529 plan is a tax-advantaged education savings plan operated by a state or educational institution, designed to help families set aside funds for future college costs. Visit www.collegesavings.org for more information.

Thanks to Rachel's journal, she realized she really enjoyed her vegetable garden, and the kids enjoyed working in the garden too.

Together she and Leonard sketched out a plan to expand the garden, and that summer they planted enough vegetables to noticeably lower their grocery bill.

By reflecting on what was important to them and what they could do without, Rachel and Leonard made some key adjustments to their family budget and for the first time they began to feel prosperous, even though their income hadn't changed.

Reacting to Setbacks

Things are not going to go right all of the time. It is important to remember that a setback is not a failure; it's just another chance to prove how strong and determined you are. Before you begin a big undertaking, write notes of encouragement to yourself. You should have an idea of what you may face, so it's a good idea to write yourself a note to help you deal with obstacles. It's sometimes easier to give and receive advice when you are in a relaxed state of mind. Write yourself notes and seal them in an envelope with a title of "In case of _____, open envelope." Write a brief note to yourself and remind yourself why you are doing what you are doing. Be sure to heed your own advice. If you cannot trust yourself, who can you trust?

Setbacks come in all shapes and sizes. Sometimes a setback can be significant and cause a tremendous disruption. An unfortunate fact, which I mentioned earlier in this book, is that the biggest cause of personal bankruptcy is unexpected medical expenses. Other leading causes of bankruptcy are job loss, divorce, natural disaster, and misuse of credit cards.

On the road of prosperity, there are three kinds of setbacks. Let's discuss them and what you can do to prevent them. They are:

Self-induced. This type of setback is entirely within your control. The best way to correct course is to admit your mistake, regroup, and get back on the Prosperity Track. Thankfully, the ability to correct course is also within your control.

James was married with two great kids, and the family was able to make ends meet. Everything was fine until one day shortly after James turned thirty-five years old; he had what many people call a midlife crisis. On that day, he woke up, went to the bathroom mirror, and saw the first evidence of grey hair around his temples. Although his wife Kelly thought he looked handsome, James was horrified.

That same day, during his lunch break, he went to look at sports cars. He found a mint condition sports car for sixty thousand dollars, bought it, and drove it home that same day. His kids were thrilled, but Kelly nearly had a heart attack. In her opinion, her husband's purchase was the most irresponsible thing either of them had ever done. But being a wise wife and knowing her husband, she held her tongue until after dinner. She gently suggested to James that while the sports car was beautiful and fun, it really wasn't something they could afford. After returning to reality, James understandably agreed. Then she had a brilliant idea: why not go on a weekend trip along the coast in a *rented* sports car? So the next day James returned the car (the dealer, having seen these episodes before, was not surprised to see him). A few weeks later James and Kelly rented an exotic sports car for five hundred dollars, spent a weekend on the coast, and had a fun and memorable time for a total cost under two thousand dollars. The vacation cost them less than two payments to the fancy sports car James originally brought home.

This completely self-induced setback resulted in a treasured experience for James and Kelly. By being realistic, they were able to avoid a detour and stay on the road of prosperity. And the next time Kelly was tempted to splurge on an expensive designer dress, she remembered what a good sport her husband had been about the car, and decided to wait until the dress went on sale.

Predictable and preventable. The second type of setback is one that is foreseeable and can be prevented with proper planning.

For example, you know that someday you are going to either retire or be unable to work. The process of aging has happened to every human being in history and, if you're lucky, it's going to happen to you too. Therefore, you can't claim ignorance of what's ahead. While it's hard for anyone to imagine themselves as being old, it's better than the alternative.

Sometimes people foolishly gamble with their current prosperity. Kevin owned a beach house located on the Gulf Coast. It wasn't just near the beach; it was on the beach. Kevin could step out of his back door and be ankle deep in the warm sand. The surf lapped against his little private dock just a few yards away. It was a lovely location and the sunsets were glorious.

The house was also dead center on the annual hurricane path. Yet year after year, Kevin didn't bother getting insurance to cover the house in case of flood or wind damage. He felt the insurance was too expensive. It's true; insurance for hurricanes is very expensive. Each year, Kevin just crossed his fingers and hoped he'd be one of the lucky ones. As the years rolled by, Kevin actually thought he was on the Prosperity Track. He had enough money to pay his bills and was living the life he always dreamed of. So why worry?

You probably guessed what happened next. One night a hurricane obliterated Kevin's beachfront home and reduced it to kindling. Kevin escaped with his life but with little else. He had no insurance, and for Kevin the road of prosperity came to an abrupt end. To his credit, he got motivated. He moved into a small apartment farther inland, sold the now-vacant beachfront lot, and after a few months managed to get back on the Prosperity Track. But it had been an expensive and unnecessary lesson.

Risky investments are another common source of avoidable setbacks. While it's true that every investment carries some chance of failure, any financial advisor will tell you that if you're making a high-risk investment—say, into a company that has never been profitable—you'd better be able to afford losing your entire investment. If you can't afford to lose, you shouldn't invest in the first place.

Risky investments don't just happen on Wall Street; they can happen on Main Street too. Richard and Dorothy were doing well and were on the road of prosperity when Dorothy's brother Jack called. Jack was opening a new restaurant and was looking for investors. He asked Richard and Dorothy to lend him ten thousand dollars. According to Jack, the restaurant concept was a sure-fire winner, and they'd get paid back within a year with interest.

Dorothy knew her brother—he was a charming, charismatic guy, but prone to exaggerate. The odds of the restaurant being a success, and investors earning a return, were slim to none. She and her husband felt trapped, but what could they do? To refuse Jack outright would create tension within the family. So Dorothy and Richard reviewed their finances and determined how much could they afford to lose, should the restaurant fail. They also considered how much they could recover from the sale the restaurant's assets if it did indeed fail. After reviewing their position, they agreed to loan Jack five thousand dollars.

Needless to say, the assets of the failed restaurant were sold at auction and Richard and Dorothy recovered two thousand dollars. Their financial setback had cost them three thousand dollars, which wasn't pleasant, but it was an amount they could afford to lose. Eventually Jack managed to open a restaurant that made money and paid his sister back, restoring harmony within the family. By planning ahead for a potential setback, Dorothy and Richard stayed on the Prosperity Track.

Unpredictable and unpreventable. The third category of setbacks are unforeseeable events that have the potential to cripple prosperity. A sudden illness is the most common, followed by an unpredictable natural disaster, an accident, or job loss. Fortunately, in our society we have organizations that provide some relief from some unforeseen setbacks. Health insurance can cover some of the costs of illness or accident; unemployment insurance exists for individuals who have lost their job through no fault of their own; and federal disaster relief funds are often available to communities that have been hit by natural disasters. Despite these resources, a major unforeseen calamity can throw you off the Prosperity Track. How you respond is up to you; assuming you are in good health and can resume earning money, often it's just a matter of time before you can rebuild your life. You may have to re-invent your vision of prosperity. For example, if you've been laid off, you may have difficulty finding a job in the same industry, and may have to get trained to work in an industry that's hiring. In our current economy, jobs in health care are increasing, as are jobs in high-tech manufacturing. Meanwhile, jobs in government, transportation, and hospitality are declining. Career colleges are working overtime to train workers for the growing job sectors.

When recovering from a serious setback, it helps to have support from family, friends, and your community. Anyone who has faced a personal crisis has said outside support and encouragement made a huge difference in the speed and impact of their recovery. You can "pay it forward" by being helpful to someone who needs it, because if a disaster happens to you, you'll appreciate it in return.

Tackling Excuses

We all have excuses why things didn't work out for us. To the person speaking it's a reason; to the person listening it's an excuse. As an exercise, the next time you face a challenge, think about the advice you would give your best friend if it happened to them. Would you tell them to give up and move on? Or would you remind them of the task's importance and encourage them to be strong?

Unfortunately, we give ourselves excuses most frequently. When evaluating potential actions or purchases, we have the unique ability of talking ourselves into a decision (usually against our better judgment). We tend to focus on the reasons why we should buy something rather than the reasons why we shouldn't. Most often, people slip off their budgets because of an impulse purchase. Here are some common excuses given for such missteps:

It was on sale. The logic here is when buying an expensive item at a discount, you're actually "saving" money. For example, Susan bought a five hundred dollar purse that was marked down to three hundred dollars. She told her husband she had saved two hundred dollars. "Yes," replied her husband, "but we *spent* three hundred dollars to *save* two hundred dollars!" In reality, had the purse been full price, she never would have bought it.

I needed to make myself feel good. How many times do we spend money just to make ourselves feel better? If we have a bad day, we head to the mall and buy something. The good feelings created by spending money have nothing to do with solving the problem that made us unhappy, and chances are we're going to buy something we don't really need. Exercise, music, and time spent with friends are excellent alternatives to shopping. And best of all, these things are free!

I wanted to celebrate. The flip side to the previous example is buying when we feel euphoric. This typically comes after we've received some monetary gain like a raise at work, but it can also be for trivial reasons. If you want to celebrate a victory or a milestone in life, that's great, but make sure the reward fits within your finances. Tommy was a fun guy, beloved by his co-workers. Whenever he was awarded his quarterly sales bonus, he would celebrate with a night out on the town. His lavish night of exquisite food, delicious cocktails, and amazing entertainment would often cost the amount of his bonus. After examining why he was not achieving prosperity, he chose to reduce his celebrations to a more reasonable level. After adjusting his rewards, he was back on the Prosperity Track.

It was an once-in-a-lifetime opportunity. Charles loved classic wines, so when a bottle of 1947 Cheval Blanc became available he was ready to buy it for a cool fifty thousand dollars. He was briefly happy until his accountant told him he'd have to dip into his retirement account for cash and postpone his plans to renovate the guest bedroom for his wife's art studio. Better sense prevailed, and instead of buying the bottle, Charles started a wine fund. A few years later another bottle of 1947 Cheval Blanc became available, and because he was still on the Prosperity Track, he was able to use the money in his wine fund to buy the bottle.

I can afford it. We often consider purchases within the context of how much we earn before taxes. We should think about purchases relative to our weekly or monthly budget. Looking at spending this way may help you make better decisions with your money. Too many times, people think they can afford something because there is enough room on their credit card or they can make the monthly payment. Impulse purchases and monthly payments are okay as long as they are built into your budget and they don't derail your goals. Unfortunately, too many people buy cars they can't afford. They can make the payments, unfortunately at the expense of saving or by using their credit cards for other purchases. If you have to charge your groceries in order to have enough money available to make your car payment, it's too expensive!

I work hard. This one is my favorite! This excuse is the ultimate "trump card" or "get out of jail free card." When all else fails, and you know you shouldn't buy something, this is the last line of defense. This excuse gives immediate credibility to whatever you want to do. Unfortunately, this is a terrible excuse. In all of my years, I have never met anyone who thought they didn't work hard. As an experiment, ask the laziest person at work if they work hard. You will receive a resounding "Yes" every time! Unfortunately, hard work has very little to do with affordability. But, affordability has everything to do with your income and expenses.

Chapter Six Takeaways

Goals can be a wonderful tool to motivate us and keep us on the Prosperity Track. Unfortunately, most people set goals and never develop a plan to achieve them. As I mentioned earlier, a goal without a plan is just a wish. Several things can help make your plan work:

- Review your income and expenses; understand which expenses are wants and which are needs.
- Determine whether your expenses are improving or hindering your prosperity.
- Develop a plan that leads to prosperity.

- Don't let a temporary setback derail your prosperity journey.
- Consider whether you are making an excuse or providing a reason.

With some soul searching and hard work, you will formulate a plan to achieve your vision of prosperity. Financial stress can be debilitating, yet prosperity requires a feeling of empowerment. Make a plan to improve your wellbeing.

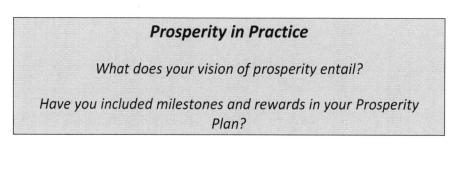

Prosperity in Practice

What does your vision of prosperity entail?

Have you included milestones and rewards in your Prosperity Plan?

Prosperity in Action

Write in your journal every day for the next thirty days.

Review your flashcards every week.

Create a prosperity plan each month for the next three months.

Chapter Seven

Implementing the Plan

> *"How soon 'not now' becomes 'never'."*
> **Martin Luther**

Success in life, they say, is eighty percent planning and twenty percent execution. In Chapters One through Five, I revealed the importance of laying the groundwork for your journey on the Prosperity Track. We discussed how prosperity is not about reaching a number or keeping up with the Joneses, but a reflection of your values and your aspirations for the quality of life for you and your family. Thus far, we have defined prosperity, learned what it takes to become prosperous, set goals, and make smart choices. In Chapter Six, you took all that you have learned and built your *Prosperity Plan*. In Chapter Seven, you will implement this plan.

Be careful, the Prosperity Track is long and winding, and full of obstacles and temptations. To stay on track requires self-discipline and a commitment to your goals. And above all, as you travel on the

Prosperity Track, you'll remember that the true essence of prosperity is:

The personal state of achievement, contentment, and wellbeing.

Whatever helps you to remain in this state is a positive force, and whatever pulls you away from this state needs to be carefully evaluated for its negative effects. These are the choices life presents us. Our lives are shaped by the choices we make. Even though events outside of our control can change our circumstances, how we react is our choice. We must first accept responsibility for our actions and recognize that we have the ability to shape our own destiny.

Remember that your *Prosperity Plan* is an evolving document. It needs to be followed consistently, although it's not set in stone. It evolves over time as your circumstances change. Your interests may change as you get older, your household budget may change throughout your career, you may need to pay for your children's college tuition, or setbacks such as an illness may require you to alter your plan.

I have included some key concepts you need to understand and put into practice in order to move forward.

Include Others

Before we begin, let's talk about the power of united action. While the idea of managing your life like a lone explorer may seem appealing—we all like to be self-sufficient—in reality you'll achieve much better results if you involve family members or friends along the Prosperity Track. When it comes to achieving goals, nothing is more motivating than sharing your goals with someone else. We are quick to break a promise to ourselves, but not to others. We regularly let ourselves down with utter disappointment, but eventually let ourselves off the hook. However, when we tell someone else, we become immediately accountable to that person. This is a powerful paradigm shift. We hate the feeling of having someone disappointed in us; it can be devastating. Avoiding feelings of failure and disappointment can be great motivation along the Prosperity Track.

Revealing our goals and our plan to achieve those goals to others can bring us several benefits. They include:

Encouragement – Our trusted friends, family, and colleagues often cheer us on when things get tough. This helps us persevere and continue on our journey. People will naturally check in with you to see how your journey is progressing. This attention can energize you to forge ahead and achieve prosperity.

Support – No one person has all the answers. Sometimes it's important to ask for help and support from others. No one ever accomplished greatness on their own; somewhere along the way they got help. Help from others with a different point of view will enable you to become better than you can be on your own. Support will help you progress further and faster than you have ever imagined.

Accountability – Being accountable is the strongest factor in achieving our goals. When someone else is involved, we work harder. For example, if we know someone is meeting us at the gym, we are much more likely to go. A sense of accountability will empower you to do things you normally would not try.

For a married couple or life partners, sharing goals with each other is very important. You cannot possibly succeed in making prosperity-focused decisions if your spouse or partner is working in the opposite direction. You need to work as a team. Other relevant family members—siblings, parents, and children—should be involved too. Their life experiences will benefit you, their encouragement will keep you going, and being accountable to them will help keep you on track.

Involving others may be as simple as being honest. For example, Jason's buddies occasionally ribbed him about his old beat-up car. They constantly wondered why he didn't get a new one. Finally, Jason told them that he didn't buy a new car because he was spending his money on evening classes. He was earning his master's degree to qualify for higher-paying management positions. He told his buddies that when he got a higher-paying job he'd be happy to buy a new car. After Jason told his friends about his goal of graduating, they stopped pressuring him to buy a new car and even encouraged him to finish school. By setting a tangible reward and including his friends, Jason increased the likelihood of accomplishing his goal to graduate. Through sharing his goals, he was able to turn a negative influence positive. And by aligning his free time and hard-earned money with his vision of prosperity, he was able to stay on the Prosperity Track.

Create a Checklist

Go back to your goal flashcards and select a few goals to which you are truly committed. Brainstorm and build a checklist of the things you will do to feel prosperous. Visually making progress on your checklist will keep you on track and moving forward. If you ever feel lost or as if you are going nowhere, refer to your checklist. Checklists should be continually updated to make sure you remain on the Prosperity Track.

For example, let's say that Rebecca's three primary goals are to:

1. Live comfortably in a nice neighborhood.
2. Enjoy good health.
3. Travel the world and explore exotic places that tourists don't normally go.

Goals #1 and #2 are what I call ubiquitous goals. These goals are commonly shared by most people. Other ubiquitous goals may include having an interesting career, raising a family, or taking part in the community. You'll notice that Rebecca's goals don't say anything about her career. To Rebecca, it doesn't much matter what she does for work; presumably, she'll follow any career path for which she's qualified and which pays well. While some people live to work, Rebecca works to live. Rebecca works as a legal assistant in a big law firm, and while it's work she enjoys, she may consider moving up in the firm.

Goal #3 is Rebecca's personal goal. While many people would welcome a trip around the world, few people share this exact goal. For

Rebecca, it's how she measures her happiness and the quality of her life. If she's able to travel the world freely, she considers herself prosperous.

Eventually Rebecca may add a fourth goal: to develop a career that allows her to travel the world as part of her job, perhaps as a tour director or perhaps an international legal consultant. It's ideal if you can align your passion with your profession. That may happen to Rebecca one day, but for now, the three key things she wants are to live in a nice neighborhood, enjoy good health, and travel the world. Rebecca is willing to make a long-term commitment to these goals forsaking some interests in the process.

Other personal goals may include writing a novel, learning a foreign language, being able to play golf every week, living on the beach, or finding a cure for cancer. It's whatever a prosperous and meaningful life means to you.

The next step is to figure out what you need to do to achieve each one of your goals. What are the specific requirements of each goal? Let's see what Rebecca might put on her list.

Live comfortably in a nice neighborhood. Basically, Rebecca wants a safe and secure place to live while she's working towards her next trip abroad, and wants her home to be secure while she's gone. She isn't particularly interested in being a homeowner, because that takes more responsibility than renting. As the years go by, that may change—remember that goals and priorities change over time—but right now, she just wants a place that's homey and secure. She needs an apartment in a good building. In order to afford a decent apartment, she needs $1,000 a month for rent. For someone else, a comfortable and secure place may mean a house in the suburbs. For someone who rides horses, it may be a farm in the country with a stable.

Good health. Another ubiquitous goal, but for Rebecca it's particularly important because she likes to travel to exotic places where there is an increased risk of disease. She needs to take care of herself physically, which includes a gym membership, vitamins, and a top-notch health plan. For these items, she'll budget $500 a month.

Travel the world. This will require money. Let's say that Rebecca is able to travel for four weeks out of the year. Including global transportation, each week abroad will cost her $2,000. So she'll budget $8,000 for travel every year.

When she adds up her other living expenses—car, food, clothing, retirement plan, and all the normal stuff people buy—Rebecca figures she needs to earn $45,000 a year. Fortunately, her job as a legal assistant pays $50,000 a year. Although her income exceeds her spending, there's not much room for error. Plus, Rebecca needs to pay down some lingering credit card debt.

Having deepened our understanding of her goals, the next step is to make a checklist of action steps needed to achieve those goals. Here's Rebecca's checklist:

1. Earn $50,000 a year or more at Smith & Smith Law Firm.
2. Maintain good health for $500 per month = $6,000 per year.
3. Rent an apartment in a safe neighborhood for $1,000 per month = $12,000 per year.

4. Buy an economical car and keep it long after the loan is repaid. Pay $300 per month for sixty months, and then keep the car five more years. Payments = $3,600 per year for five years.

5. Pay $300 per month for fifteen months to eliminate expensive credit card debt = $3,600 per year for one year and three months.

6. Contribute $2,500 per year to company 401(k) account, matched by employer.

7. Save at least $8,000 per year for travel.

8. Budget $1,100 per month for taxes and living expenses = $13,200 per year.

9. Cushion of $1,100 per year for savings and emergencies. This will increase to $4,700 per year after credit cards are paid off. Some of this increase can be put towards more exotic or luxurious travel plans.

10. Get promoted to senior legal assistant with salary of $58,000 a year, giving a bigger cushion of $12,700 per year. Additional earnings can be used to pay for evening classes to earn an accounting degree. With a degree in accounting, Rebecca will qualify for even higher paying jobs.

Stages of Implementation

Unfortunately, your goals can't all be accomplished simultaneously; often they must be approached in multiple stages. A variety of short-term and long-term goals can be undertaken at the same time, or as

Larry and Monique discovered, a big long-term goal can be most easily attained by tackling a series of smaller milestones.

Now that you've made your list of goals and the action steps needed to achieve them, determine which goals have the largest impact and implement a plan to accomplish these first. Next, select small attainable goals to gain confidence and momentum. Amongst your goals, pick a few that have an immediate impact with little effort. Remember the categories of goals I presented in Chapter Four:

A. Short-term and easy.
B. Short-term and challenging.
C. Long-term and easy.
D. Long-term and challenging.

Larry and Monique had one big long-term goal: to save $33,000 for a down payment on a house. They had $15,000 saved and needed $18,000 more. They broke down the single "long term and challenging" goal into a series of "short term and easy" goals of saving $1,100 before giving themselves a reward.

Prosperity is not always about money. You can have millions in the bank and not lead a life of prosperity. Your personal *Prosperity Plan* may include many non-monetary components that reflect your quality of life—anything from visiting your mother more often to climbing Mt. Everest. While some of your goals may require generating more income or reducing expenses, others have nothing to do with money.

If possible, plan to accomplish or make progress on your goals daily. For sixty days, you can set small daily tasks you will accomplish the following day. Each statement can be written in your journal to acknowledge what you have achieved and what you will accomplish next. Here is a sample format:

"Today, I _____(verb)_____ (noun) and tomorrow, I will _____ (verb)_____(noun)." For example, "Today, I cleaned my garage, and tomorrow I will learn five new Spanish words."

Sometimes we need to get back on the road of prosperity after experiencing a major change in our lives. Adele was happily married for thirty-five years, but then her husband unexpectedly passed away. Adele was devastated, and once she recovered from her immediate grief, she realized she didn't quite know what to do with herself. She spent most of her adult life facilitating her husband's successful career and hadn't spent much time developing her own interests. Although her husband left her with enough money to maintain her current lifestyle, she didn't feel prosperous. Her life was empty, not just because she had lost her husband, but because she didn't have any personal goals. After much soul searching, she decided to begin living her life to the fullest, choosing to engage in activities that brought her personal satisfaction and joy.

She made some goals to get her back on the Prosperity Track. Here they are:

1. Get the vegetable garden in shape.
2. Learn how to make silver jewelry.
3. Complete the volunteer training program at the local hospital.
4. Take a course in financial planning to better manage my money.
5. Visit Italy—particularly the art centers of Rome and Florence.
6. Learn to speak Italian to make the trip more fun and rewarding.
7. Visit my two children more often.

Some of Adele's goals were short-term (the vegetable garden took one weekend of intense activity) while others were long-term, such as learning how to make silver jewelry. As the months passed, Adele reviewed and modified her goals. After a year, she had amended her list to look like this:

1. Get the vegetable garden in shape.
   Done!
2. Learn how to make silver jewelry.
   Taking a course with a local silversmith.
3. Complete the volunteer training program at the local hospital.
   Done – now I volunteer three days a week.
4. Take a course in financial planning to better manage my money.
   Done!

5. Visit Italy—particularly the art centers of Rome and Florence.

    Trip planned for next month with college alumni group.

6. Learn to speak Italian to make the trip more fun and rewarding.

    I took an evening class at the community college.

7. Visit my two children more often.

    Ongoing.

8. Join the board of directors of the local art museum.

9. Remodel the kitchen—take up the old linoleum floor and put down hardwood, and replace the old cabinets.

10. Explore the possibility of opening my own jewelry store.

As you can see, Adele completed some of her goals, with others still in progress. She was also able to add three new goals, including one significant long-term goal: open her own jewelry store selling her own handmade pieces and other items made by local skilled artisans. Part of her motivation for opening her own store was to keep herself busy doing something she loved, but to also generate some additional cash flow.

Proactively Manage Your Budget

As we saw with Adele, your goals are likely to evolve over time. Problems get solved, goals are met, and new challenges may present themselves. A major change in your life—divorce, death of a spouse or partner, illness, or even a big raise in salary at work—can trigger a shift in your priorities. Sometimes the change will be purely financial, and other times, like with Adele, the change will be personal.

Just as your list of goals needs to be actively maintained and updated, so does your household budget. Debts get paid, incomes change, and opportunities arise necessitating regular updates. When adjustments need to be made, you have three choices:

1. *Increase income.* If you don't have enough income to reach prosperity, brainstorm actions you can take to generate additional income, even if only temporarily. There are many ways to increase your income, including getting a promotion at your current place of employment, finding a higher paying job, or establishing a side business.

2. *Decrease spending.* If you are not saving enough money, you may need to reduce expenses. Expense management is important on the Prosperity Track. Determine which expenses can be reduced or eliminated without a detriment to your health and wellbeing. Make trial expense reductions to see what results are obtained.

3. *Financial engineering.* Look at your expenses and see if there are lower cost options for things you are already doing. See if you qualify for multi-line discounts with your insurance carriers. Compare insurance policy rates with other reputable providers. Inquire about refinancing your mortgage at a lower rate. If you have credit card debt, call the company and see if there are better rates available. If you have car loans, check to see if you are able to refinance at a lower rate. Although these

tactics take effort on your part, they're important because the monthly savings can really add up.

Joseph and Rosita were happily married with two young children. Joseph worked as an editor at a large corporation, while Rosita was a business consultant. Juggling their two workdays plus the kids was a challenge. They felt their quality of life was not what it could have been. Joseph and Rosita's work schedules were drastically different and they saw less of each other than they wanted. Their household felt like a solar system with four planets always orbiting but never meeting! But they stuck with the arrangement because they felt financially secure.

Then disaster struck: Joseph was laid off from his job. His $70,000-a-year salary was gone. What were they going to do?

Joseph and Rosita sat down at their kitchen table and took a hard look at their situation. Joseph's company had given him two months' salary as severance pay, after which he would be eligible for state unemployment benefits. If they made no changes to their budget, they could live for six months using their emergency fund. If after six months Joseph wasn't making enough income, they'd have to use his 401k account, which would be subject to taxes and penalties. A change in circumstances often results in new options. Joseph felt he could make a change for the betterment of his family. He had often contemplated becoming a freelance editor, working from home. He didn't particularly enjoy working at a big company; it had been a job he had just sort of fallen into after college. The family still had Rosita's health plan to cover their medical issues, which allowed additional flexibility. Joseph proposed he could stay home with the kids and develop his own online freelance editing business. An added economic benefit emerged—a stay-at-home dad—would eliminate the need to pay for day care, which would save them $1,000 each month.

Initially, Rosita wasn't sure about taking over the role of chief breadwinner. After a couple nights of discussion and contemplation, she was willing to try it for a few months. Joseph set up his office in the spare room, and the next week the kids didn't go to daycare, but went happily marching to the playground with their dad. Joseph soon got the knack for organizing playdates with friends, which was a huge benefit. True, when the playdates were at their house, he was overwhelmed by the toddler-filled house, but when they visited a friend's home, he was able to concentrate on his work.

Joseph and Rosita adjusted their family's monthly income budget to reflect their new reality:

- Rosita's salary = $3,500 per month (unchanged).
- Joseph's unemployment insurance = $2,250 (will last only twenty-six weeks, or about six and a half months, and is taxable).
- Savings from canceling daycare = $1,000 per month.

Before Joseph was laid off, the family had earned $102,000 a year, or about $8,500 a month. For the next twenty-six weeks their income would be Rosita's salary ($3,500) plus Joseph's unemployment benefits ($2,250) totaling $5,750 per month. That's a loss of $2,750 per month. But with Joseph at home, they would be saving $1,000 a month in childcare costs, so the income gap was reduced to $1,750 a month. Their savings could cover this gap for six months.

The question for Joseph was how fast could he generate income with his new business? Could he find clients and get paying jobs that would make up the gap within six months?

Joseph and Rosita took a chance, but within a year, the family was nearly breaking even. After five years, Joseph was making as much as he made at his corporate job. Both he and Rosita were happier, and the family was back on the Prosperity Track.

Tiptoe to Prosperity

Prosperity does not happen overnight. Small steps must be made in the quest for prosperity. With each new step, you get closer to your prosperous life. Although each step may be insignificant if examined on its own, collectively they are powerful. Just because something doesn't have a large immediate impact doesn't mean it isn't worthwhile. Focus on what is important and work towards it. Small gradual steps taken consecutively with purpose will lead you to prosperity. Consistency is the key. When you look back, you will be able to see just how far you've come in a short period of time. Now that is extremely positive motivation.

The road ahead is tough, but making a number of small changes can lead to big results. It's important to recognize that you are making progress and getting closer to where you want to be. Most people quit things when they don't see immediate results. Be patient!

You will be amazed at the ground you gain when you master your expenses. Most people with credit card debt have a hard time explaining where the debt came from. They can't put their finger on any one expense that attributed to the majority of their balance. Usually it's many small charges that accumulated over time. Revisit expenses like: smoking, eating out, gym memberships you don't use, magazine subscriptions you don't read, cable channels you don't watch, ATM fees, house cleaning, car washes, lawn care, etc. I am not telling you to eliminate them (unless you are in a drastic financial situation), but you should investigate whether you can save money by adjusting the frequency, program, or vendor.

The Tools of the Trade

Managing your money is more than just making wise spending choices. It's also about what to do with the money you have—how to keep more of it, lose less of it, and make it grow. There are many different tools you can use to help you get on the road of prosperity and keep you there. Although a deep explanation of financial planning is beyond the scope of this book, there are some tools you should be aware of:

Insurance – Make sure your family has ample protection in case of an unforeseen event. Some people have no coverage or too little coverage. Insurance is a competitive industry; shop around to find the proper coverage and pricing. Make sure you choose a reputable company when purchasing insurance. Check out the insurance company's ratings with A.M. Best at www.ambest.com and do an internet search to read about other customers' experiences. If it sounds too good to be true, it probably is.

Investments – Investment opportunities exist in stocks, bonds, real estate, commodities, etc. Make investments appropriate for your goals, comfort level, and risk tolerance. Just because an investment has performed well in the past does not mean it will in the future. Not every investment is appropriate for every investor, regardless of its return potential.

Taxes – Unless you have an ultra-simple tax return, work with an experienced and qualified tax professional. Don't lose dollars by trying to save pennies. Taxpayers don't always take full advantage of the tax code. If you owe taxes, pay them before you pay any other debt. Tax debt is extremely expensive and the government—city, state, or federal—can seize your bank and retirement accounts if you don't pay.

Savings/spending accounts – There are special accounts created for specific goals. Each has a set of benefits, costs, and considerations. When appropriate use vehicles designed for specific goals.

- ○ *Retirement* – 401k, 403b, 457, IRAs, etc. should be used as a retirement savings account and not for the purchase of anything else. Although the funds can be accessed through loans or paying penalties, this is rarely a good idea. This money is targeted for retirement and should only be accessed for that purpose or in case of dire emergencies. Beware of taxes and penalties for early withdrawal.

- o *College* – 529, UTMA, UGMA, Educational IRAs, and prepaid tuition programs are designed for higher education, they offer lots of positives. Make sure you do your due diligence regarding fees and investments before beginning any program.

- o *Brokerage* – After tax investment accounts are good for intermediate goals and emergency funds. Brokerage accounts can hold a wide variety of investments, such as: CDs, stocks, bonds, mutual funds, exchange traded funds (ETFs), etc. Be sure to compare different providers. Look for a large reputable company with no annual fees and low commissions.

- o *Checking/savings accounts* – Great for everyday expenses and emergency funds. Consider features, benefits, and costs. It's a very competitive industry, so shop around. Beware of sneaky fees. ATM, low balance, monthly maintenance, and per check fees can cost you hundreds of dollars a year.

- o *Debit/credit cards* – Consider fees and expenses. It's best to use a debit card so you can track your expenses online, as I discussed in Chapter Five under "Budgeting." Compare credit card interest rates and incentive programs. Find the best credit card that fits your usage.

○ *Cash* – Use sparingly. Paying with cash is hard to track and often leads to impulse spending. Cash can also be dangerous to carry.

The above tools can be intimidating and very confusing. Sometimes it's hard to know whom to trust. Spend some time educating yourself. You shouldn't aim to be an expert, but rather to learn enough to make an informed decision. Remember—buyer beware. If it sounds too good to be true, it most likely is. One last cliché—there is no free lunch. Remember that companies are in business to make profits, somewhere along the way they need to get paid. I am not against anyone earning a fair profit from providing a product or service to a customer. What I am against is the fly by night charlatans who are after a quick buck at the direct expense of a trusting customer. When making decisions about your financial wellbeing, take the time to learn, think, and make an informed decision.

Chapter Seven Takeaways

Implementing your *Prosperity Plan* will be the most important step along the Prosperity Track. All the time and effort spent defining prosperity, envisioning your ideal lifestyle, identifying your current position, establishing prosperity goals, and developing your *Prosperity Plan* will all be wasted unless you put what you have learned into practice. Be proactive and commit to your own prosperity. Share your *Prosperity Plan* with family and friends; they can be great allies along the Prosperity Track. Learn about the tools that can help you succeed along your journey. The time is now to take what you have learned and forge ahead.

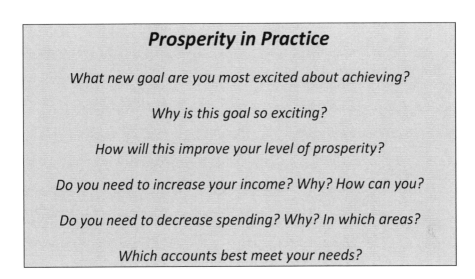

Prosperity in Practice

What new goal are you most excited about achieving?

Why is this goal so exciting?

How will this improve your level of prosperity?

Do you need to increase your income? Why? How can you?

Do you need to decrease spending? Why? In which areas?

Which accounts best meet your needs?

Prosperity in Action

Create your checklist. Monitor and update it regularly.

Get in the habit of setting small daily tasks.

Investigate the best accounts for your needs.

Chapter Eight

Monitor and Adjust

"I can't change the direction of the wind, but I can adjust my sails to always reach my destination."

Jimmy Dean

Congratulations for creating and implementing your personal *Prosperity Plan*! I hope you're energized and excited to begin your journey, and are on the road of prosperity or at least approaching the on-ramp.

In order to stay on the Prosperity Track, you need to remember two concepts. The first important thing you must do is focus on your vision of prosperity and the goals needed to achieve it. Remember the definition of prosperity I suggested:

The personal state of achievement, contentment, and wellbeing.

How you define these three conditions is up to you, but I encourage you to consider them not in monetary terms but in terms of your quality of life. In order to reach your goals you will no doubt have to generate income and manage your budget, but these are a means to an end, not an end themselves. Your vision of prosperity may be a remote cabin in the woods, or perhaps a mansion on the seashore with a mega-yacht tied at the dock. It may be running your own one-person freelance company, or it may be serving as the CEO of a multinational corporation. Prosperity may be teaching English to schoolchildren in Kenya or being the president of a large university. Whatever it is, your vision of prosperity should be that which brings you personal achievement, contentment, and wellbeing.

To stay on the Prosperity Track, the second most important concept to remember is prosperity is a process. It's not a destination in the sense that once you have arrived you are forever "safe." The unfortunate reality is prosperity can be lost more quickly than it can be gained.

You may know of country superstar Willie Nelson, but you may not know how close he came to having his prosperous lifestyle wiped out. After Willie had built a successful career as a Nashville songwriter, the critical success of his 1973 album *Shotgun Willie* followed by the critical and commercial success of *Red Headed Stranger* (1975) and *Stardust* (1978) made him one of the most recognized artists in country music. In the late 1970s and through the 1980s, Willie experienced prosperity and the satisfaction of having control over his career and his life.

Then in 1990, Willie's assets were seized by the Internal Revenue Service, which claimed he owed the government back taxes. Many of his tax problems involved his accountants having invested heavily in tax shelters ruled illegal by the IRS. Between his original unpaid taxes and interest and penalties, Willie owed the IRS more than $16 million. Although his lawyers convinced the IRS to accept a $6 million cash payment to settle Willie's debt, this was more than he could pay. "He didn't have one million dollars. He probably didn't even have thirty thousand," his daughter, Lana Nelson, told *Texas Monthly* magazine.

In January 1991, the government auctioned his home and belongings to the highest bidder. The winning bidder of his home turned out to be one of Willie's fans, who purchased the ranch at the behest of a group of farmers who had supported Willie in appreciation for his work in organizing the Farm Aid charitable concerts. Many of the personal belongings auctioned off were purchased by friends, who returned his possessions to him.

That same year Willie released *The IRS Tapes: Who'll Buy My Memories?* With the profits from the double album and the auction of Willie's assets, his debt to the IRS was satisfied. Today, Willie continues to earn money through his music, songwriting, roles in television and films, and writing. He wrote his autobiography and several other books. Today he's estimated to have a net worth of $15 million.

It was a close call for Willie Nelson, who perhaps relied too much on dubious tax advice from accountants who were mismanaging his assets. Through hard work and discipline, he was able to get back on the Prosperity Track. Thankfully, his experiences taught him a valuable lesson in money management that would serve him well in the future.

Track Your Prosperity

What can you do to stay on the road of prosperity? The most important thing you can do is to maintain a keen awareness of both your current position and where you're headed. Here are my top four tips for staying on the Prosperity Track:

1. *Educate yourself.* As you can see from the example of Willie Nelson, sometimes reliance on so-called experts can still lead to disaster. You need to be educated, and if something sounds too good to be true (such as the idea that investing in "tax shelters" will reduce your income tax to zero) it probably is. Know where you're invested and the level of risk involved. If your investment advisor recommends putting a significant portion of your savings into any single investment, get a second opinion!

2. *Assess risk.* It's as foolish to keep all of your money in a box under your bed, as it is to invest it all in your cousin's startup company. Smart investors spread their exposure to a variety of areas. You should also consider liquidity; you should have some assets which can be sold quickly to raise cash should the need arise. Be sure to keep some cash in the bank for quick access in case of emergencies. However, long term hoarding

of cash and CD's can result in a decline in purchasing power due to inflation.

3. ***Stay on track.*** Once you're on your way to prosperity, don't be tempted to splurge on a major purchase that can derail your prosperity. Special purchases—things like vacations, new cars, toys such as snowmobiles, or expensive jewelry—must be made from a designated savings account. These purchases must not affect your ability to pay your bills on time or maintain your personal savings schedule. Revisit and revise your goals and actions to best support your vision of prosperity.

4. ***Save windfall monies.*** If you happen to get a big bonus from work or receive a significant gift, don't squander it. Take this "free money" and either use it to pay down debt (such as your mortgage) or put it with your savings and investments. Paying down debt may not seem like much fun since you may not see any immediate benefit. But the benefits will be noticeable when your debt is cleared quickly, and you discover you've paid less in interest than originally anticipated. Plus you can reallocate the money saved from interest payments to other areas.

Peter and Sarah did a good job of getting on the Prosperity Track. They shared a clear idea of what prosperity meant to them. They envisioned a ranch in the rolling hills with livestock and orchards. The ranch would be paid for by Peter's income from his work as a management consultant, while Sarah would oversee the operations of the ranch, which would also produce income. After five years of marriage, they realized their dream and purchased a thousand-acre spread by a scenic river. Together they created budgets detailing income and expenses, and systematically tackled both short-term and long-term goals using checklists.

Then, while experiencing financial security, a business acquaintance of Peter's suggested they invest in a new mall development. It looked like a certain success, so instead of investing a modest amount, Peter and Sarah sold most of their income producing investments and used the cash to purchase a big stake in the development. It was a risky move but their business acquaintance insisted they couldn't lose. But as the project neared completion, the region experienced a recession, and the expected tenants for the mall backed out. The storefronts remained empty and unleased for months. The developer went bankrupt and the investment was sold off for pennies on the dollar. Peter and Sarah lost their entire stake. Had they stayed on the Prosperity Track and made a reasonable investment with cash they could afford to lose, it would not have been a crisis. Their asset base had been largely depleted, and they came very close to losing their cherished ranch.

Keep Regular Worksheets

As Peter and Sarah found out, once you're on the Prosperity Track, it's important to keep your guard up. It's easy to be lulled into a false sense of security, but beware, adverse events can happen any time.

One very effective way to keep yourself on the Prosperity Track is to monitor your progress. In the early stages, you should at a minimum prepare monthly progress reports for income, expenses, and savings. Depending on your current condition and habits, you may even begin with weekly reports. By tracking your results, your decision-making process will naturally be different. When you see results from what you have been working towards, it will make it all worthwhile. This will help guide your behavior going forward.

The search for prosperity is a constant learning process that will never end. As you progress, you will move to monthly progress reports, culminating in quarterly reports. It's best to recognize potential setbacks early, so you can redirect your efforts before it's too late.

The best way to create monthly progress reports is to use your original budget, and simply note any variances from it. These variances become your current month's plan, and after the month has passed, your current month's plan then becomes your reference for next month's plan. So if this month is July, you use the version of your plan from June to compare and make adjustments.

Here's an example of a household budget created by Patricia and Kim:

Item	June	July
Mortgage	$1,500	$1,500
Car payment	350	350
Utilities	250	250
Phone and Internet	300	300
Insurance and health plan	800	800
Transportation	150	150
Food	450	450
Clothing	150	150
Entertainment	100	100
Household and personal stuff	350	350
Vacation	0	1,600
Savings	400	0
TOTAL	4,800	6,000

NET SAVINGS   ***400***   ***(1,200)***

You can see in this simplified table that Patricia and Kim's normal household budget was $4,800 per month, which included $400 put into savings. However, in July they took a one-week vacation to Mexico. Instead of depositing $400 into their savings account in July, they withdrew $1,200 from savings to help pay for the vacation that cost $1,600. The amount spent on their vacation represents four months' worth of savings.

Is there anything wrong with this? No—as long as the $1,600 vacation fits into their view of prosperity, and represents something of value to them. But let's say that Patricia is trying to open a clothing store. She needs every penny for the lease. The clothing store is very important to her and represents a lifelong dream. If this is the case, then was spending the money on a vacation a wise idea? Probably not. The money spent on vacation may have delayed accomplishing her goal of opening a store. Although fun, prioritizing their vacation may have delayed the realization of Patricia's clothing store.

Unlocking Happiness

The story of Patricia and Kim brings us to the subject I discussed in Chapter One of this book—that is, how you define prosperity and therefore happiness. The vacation Patricia and Kim took may or may not have been integral to their pursuit of prosperity. In the case of Patricia, we can suspect the vacation was not central to her idea of sustained prosperity because it hindered her goal of opening a clothing store. As she lay on the beach in Mexico, Patricia may very well have been depressed about how much time and money she was spending while on vacation and what it meant to her store opening. However, a relaxing vacation may have forced Patricia take a break from the chaos of opening the clothing store, allowing her to reenergize. She may return home with a positive attitude that could greatly increase the odds of her success.

There are many factors that determine whether we are happy or not. When we understand our guiding values, we can determine what makes us happy. When we focus on things that make us happy for the long-term rather than immediate gratification, we can unlock happiness. The ability to be happy remains inside of us yearning to be released. We all have the right to be happy, but achieving happiness is one hundred percent up to us. If we are faced with something or someone that makes us unhappy, we are responsible for making a change, not them. Expecting your circumstances to change on their own is not practical. We hold the key to unlock our happiness; we must always search for the right lock. If at first you don't find it, keep trying different locks.

Sometimes, what makes you happy and leads you onto the road of true prosperity doesn't emerge until later in life. Consider the case of best-selling author John Grisham. He was born February 8, 1955 in Jonesboro, Arkansas. As a child, John wanted to be a professional baseball player, but eventually realized he didn't have enough physical talent for a career in sports. In college, he majored in accounting at Mississippi State University, and earned his law degree from the University of Mississippi School of Law. Grisham practiced law for about a decade, focusing on personal injury and criminal defense. He dabbled in politics and was elected to the Mississippi House of Representatives, where he served from 1983 to 1990. By his second term at the Mississippi state legislature, he was the vice-chairman of the Apportionment and Elections Committee, and a member of several other committees.

With his work as a lawyer and responsibilities as a politician, he was working sixty hours a week. John's writing career began after listening to the heart-wrenching testimony of a twelve-year-old rape victim. It was during this trial Grisham considered "what would have happened if the girl's father had murdered her assailants." He began writing his novel by getting up early in the morning and writing for several hours before going to work. Grisham finished *A Time to Kill* in 1987, after three years of writing. Initially rejected by twenty-eight publishers, it was eventually bought by Wynwood Press, who published it in June 1988 with a modest press run of five thousand copies.

Such hard work and lackluster reward could have put an end to his writing, but John had discovered what made him happy. The day after he completed *A Time to Kill* he began working on his next project, the story of a talented young attorney who was "lured to an apparently perfect law firm that was not what it appeared.[2]" *The Firm* remained on *The New York Times* bestseller list for forty-seven weeks and was recognized as the bestselling novel of 1991. Except for one last appearance in court as a trial lawyer in 1996, John Grisham retired from practicing law and now lives prosperously as a novelist, having sold more than 250 million books worldwide.

What makes you happy? Could you turn it into a career?

Manage Change

Change is scary for most people. We must understand this as we progress on the Prosperity Track. There will be plenty of times when you will feel uneasy and uncomfortable. Keep your eyes on your goals and envision the prosperous lifestyle ahead of you. The power is within you to change your circumstances. Make the changes that will improve your lifestyle. The opinions and goals of others are not relevant to your track. Do what is in your heart to do.

---

[2] www.jgrisham.com/bio

Change can sometimes be life-altering. Born June 14, 1983, Jose Rene "J. R." Martinez is well-known to fans of the soap opera *All My Children*. But he doesn't look like the typical television actor; his face exhibits the disfiguring effects of a grievous battlefield injury. His long journey to his new career began when he enlisted in the US Army, and in February 2003, he was deployed to Iraq. Two months later, J.R. was driving a Humvee when its left front tire hit a roadside mine; in the violent explosion he suffered smoke inhalation and severe burns to more than thirty-four percent of his body, including his face. He was evacuated to Ramstein Air Base in Germany for immediate care and later transferred to the Army Institute of Surgical Research Burn Center at Brooke Army Medical Center ("BAMC") in San Antonio, Texas. He spent thirty-four months at BAMC and has since undergone thirty-three cosmetic and skin graft surgeries.

His ghastly injuries didn't stop him. Following his recovery, he has traveled the country as a motivational speaker, sharing his experiences with corporations, veterans groups, schools, and other organizations. In 2008, he began playing the role of Brot Monroe on the ABC daytime drama *All My Children*. He is also the winner of Season 13 of ABC's *Dancing with the Stars*. In 2008, he was honored as a "Shining Star of Perseverance" by the WillReturn Council of Assurant Employee Benefits. The following year, the nonprofit Iraq and Afghanistan Veterans of America presented him with the Veterans Leadership Award.

Hopefully, during your life you won't experience the kind of wrenching change experienced by J.R. Martinez. In fact, change most often occurs incrementally, with changes being relatively predictable.

You know that you're going to retire one day. If you have kids, you know someday they're going to start driving, graduate from high school, and eventually move out of the house. You know that technology will change, and in a few years, the spiffy new gadget you just bought will be obsolete.

Avoid Setbacks

When considering things such as retirement, you need to be particularly vigilant and engage in proactive planning. Always be proactive as you plan toward the future. If there are certain tendencies or behavioral biases you have, work with them. For example, if you are a compulsive shopper, don't go to the mall unless you have a specific item you need to buy like a birthday gift or back-to-school clothes. If you eat and drink too much with a certain group of friends, only spend time with them in controlled circumstances. If you have a propensity to gamble, stay away from casinos and people who like to gamble. Your perception is often a result of the people you choose to surround yourself with. What may seem normal within a group of peers can be anything but. Surround yourself with positive influences who share similar goals and aspirations.

Peer pressure and personal temptations can be strong. Sometimes the best course of action is to avoid circumstances likely to have negative results. It's not always the easiest track or the most fun, but it will get you where you want to go. As Bernard Baruch put it, "Those who mind don't matter and those who matter don't mind." If someone is not supportive of your new focus on improving yourself, determine whether they really have your best interests in mind. You would be surprised who wants the same things you want and yearns for someone else to share their vision. By finding someone who shares your vision, you can help each other.

Daniel landed a good job with a graphic arts company that designed websites for big corporate clients. He loved the company and enjoyed his work, but he had a secret: he was a recovering alcoholic. He was five years sober and went to Alcoholics Anonymous meetings every month for and emotional support. His wife didn't drink much and was happy to never drink in front of her husband.

The challenge for Daniel was the environment created by his coworkers. The office culture was very relaxed, and many of his colleagues enjoyed having cocktails at lunch. This was bearable, but they also enjoyed going out after work for a seemingly innocent "happy hour." Most of Daniel's office mates were single and didn't have someone waiting for them at home, so they could stay out late and carouse.

Daniel felt that his sobriety track—and therefore his Prosperity Track—was threatened. He wanted to go out after work, but felt it jeopardized his sobriety. He feared he couldn't just sit there and drink orange juice, and he was married to a wonderful woman who deserved to have him at home in the evenings. On the other hand, he wanted to be "one of the guys" and form a close bond with his colleagues, which he knew would be good for his career. Unwilling to risk a relapse, Daniel decided to avoid mixing with coworkers outside of work.

As the weeks passed, Daniel felt increasingly uncomfortable and isolated at work. And then something happened—the company's general manager left and was replaced by someone new. The new general manager had a different attitude—he was all business and expected results. With a huge sense of relief, Daniel noticed a dramatic reduction in the level of drinking at lunch and after work. He felt he could be himself and focus on his job. He was elated that his new boss's values were in closer alignment with his own.

His wife noticed the change in Daniel and told him he seemed much happier. While his income hadn't changed, Daniel's prosperity had increased because he was enjoying his job more and being a better companion to his loving wife.

Professional Advice and Services

No one person has all the answers to prosperity. Depending on your personal circumstances, for legal, lifestyle, health, and financial matters you may need assistance from a professional. Make sure you interview several different providers before making a decision. Ask for references and do some due diligence using multiple resources. Here are some examples of professionals that may aid you on your road to prosperity:

Investment advisor – Investments can be very cumbersome and confusing. If you have substantial investments, I would recommend outsourcing this activity to a professional. Whether you choose a reputable investment management company or a local advisor, select the program that best fits your needs. You should like and trust the person, but make the decision based on who will do the best job for you.

Attorney – Attorneys come in all shapes and specialties. Find the most reputable person in the field you need expertise in. Although fees are important, make your choice based largely on who you believe will provide the best results. Cheap options are often the most expensive in the long run.

Accountant/CPA – Tax errors and omissions cost taxpayers millions every year. Saving the cost of a tax preparer may require several frustrating hours and many headaches on your part. Find a reputable tax advisor to work with. Avoid people who only do taxes seasonally and are not tax experts.

Life coach – People face a number of challenges in their life and may benefit from speaking with a life coach. Life coaches help clarify life goals and may help in creating a better work-life balance.

Medical advocate – If you've had a serious illness, you may face significant bills. If you're uninsured, you will be charged a premium price for treatment, which can easily destroy your prosperity. Remember, the number one cause of personal bankruptcies in America is medical bills. If you're facing huge medical bills, locate an expert who can negotiate with the hospital and get your bill reduced.

Nutritionist – People with food allergies or medical conditions affecting their lifestyle may seek advice from a licensed nutritionist. A nutritionist can create a customized regimen based on your dietary needs and individual circumstances. The right fuel can make a huge difference in energy and mood.

Personal trainer – Exercise remains a challenge for many busy people. A qualified trainer can create a workout plan customized to fit your schedule, physical condition, and goals. People are also less likely to miss workouts when they are paying to work out with a trainer.

Physician – Make sure you're enrolled in a good health care plan and see your physician regularly. If there is something ailing you or keeping you from reaching your goals, tell your doctor. Once you identify something bothering you, take control so you can get on the track to recovery.

Psychologist/psychiatrist/family counselor – Each of us have a different history of experiences. People often benefit from speaking with a professional. If you are experiencing an emotional issue keeping you from moving ahead, look for a professional. There are many different ways to receive treatment and there is no shame in asking for help. We all face events and emotions that can overcome us with a variety of feelings. Do not let a feeling of embarrassment or shame keep you from getting the help you need.

Become a Prosperity Champion

Prosperity Champions embody all that prosperity offers. They are happy, healthy, and feel successful. They have persevered and accomplished personal greatness. Their success can help motivate others to be better and reach their full potential. Through their stories, others can hear about prosperity and learn how they too can become prosperous.

Prosperity Champions have reached a prosperous lifestyle, and may gain greater fulfillment by helping others work towards achieving their goals. Although we accomplish goals regularly, we should always be striving for something to avoid complacency and enjoy life. Here are my top three characteristics of a Prosperity Champion:

1. ***Set an example.*** Prosperity does not happen easily or quickly. People need to know and recognize what it takes. By setting a positive example, you can help others reach their fullest potential. When you share your story and challenges, others can learn from what you have experienced. Your knowledge can enable others to achieve prosperity.

2. ***Encourage others.*** Prosperity Champions can encourage and act as a sounding board to others. Newbies to the Prosperity Track will face many challenges and obstacles. A small bit of encouragement goes a long way. Encouraging others is a rewarding activity for everyone involved.

3. ***Pay it forward.*** Research has shown that people feel good when they help others. This motivates many people to volunteer time and give money to charities. I feel blessed with what I have learned and know it can benefit many others. I personally feel obligated to share what I have learned, and it makes me feel good while helping others. Helping others can truly be a win-win scenario.

Probably the most well-known Prosperity Champion in America today also happens to be one of the nation's wealthiest people: Warren Buffett. Born August 30, 1930, Warren Buffett is widely considered the most successful investor of the twentieth century. The primary shareholder, chairman, and CEO of Berkshire Hathaway who has a current net worth estimated at $54 billion, is consistently ranked among the world's wealthiest people. Known to many as the "Oracle of Omaha," he's recognized for his commitment to value investing and for his personal frugality. Buffett is also a notable philanthropist, having pledged to give away ninety-nine percent of his wealth to philanthropic endeavors, largely in partnership with the Gates Foundation.

What is interesting about Warren Buffet is that while making money is clearly very important to him, the external trappings of wealth are of little consequence. As CEO of Berkshire Hathaway, his annual salary is $100,000, which is paltry compared to the average CEO's salary of over $9 million. He lives in the same house in Dundee, Nebraska he bought in 1958 for $31,500, although he also owns a $4 million house in Laguna Beach, California. It has been reported that Buffett doesn't carry a cell phone, has no computer at his desk, and drives his own automobile.

At the beginning of his career, Warren Buffett decided what prosperity meant to him, and with single-minded determination, he followed his dream. He was not distracted by the temptations of his rapidly growing wealth and continued doing the work he enjoyed.

For others, prosperity can come after a life-changing decision. Born on February 21, 1971, Sara Blakely is the world's youngest self-made female billionaire. How did she go from being an average middle class woman to a billionaire by the age of forty? She's the founder of Spanx, the wildly successful undergarment company.

Her life story began unremarkably. Sara was born and raised in Clearwater, Florida, the daughter of a personal injury lawyer and an artist. She graduated from Florida State University with a degree in communications. She was a member of Delta Delta Delta sorority and worked part time at Walt Disney World. She joined local stationery company, Danka, and began selling fax machines door-to-door.

Her invention, like many others, started with a problem. In the heat and humidity of Florida, Sara tried unsuccessfully to find pantyhose that didn't have seamed toes and or roll up the leg when she cut them. As she says, "Working as a sales trainer by day and performing stand-up comedy at night, I didn't know the first thing about the pantyhose industry except that I dreaded wearing most pantyhose. Also, I had never taken a business class, which made the process even more challenging. As a result, I had only one source to operate from...my gut."

Investing her life savings of $5,000 in her idea for comfortable slimming hose, she moved to Atlanta, researching and trying to reach production deals with local manufacturers. Sam Kaplan, co-owner of the Charlotte, North Carolina based Highland Mills, didn't buy Blakely's pitch until polling his two daughters on what they thought of footless pantyhose. They loved the idea and said they'd buy it. Kaplan decided to take Sara's order after all, and by August 2000, she had her first three thousand pairs of hose.

In her own words: "Once I had a perfected prototype in hand, I called the buyer at Neiman Marcus and introduced myself over the phone. I said I had invented a product their customers would not want to live without, and if I could have ten minutes of her time, I would fly to Dallas. She agreed!"

"During the meeting, I had no shame. I asked her to follow me to the ladies room where I personally showed her the before/after in my cream pants. Three weeks later Spanx was on the shelves of Neiman Marcus! I did the same thing with Saks, Nordstrom, Bloomingdales, and all my other retailers."

In 2006, Sara launched the Sara Blakely Foundation to help women through education and entrepreneurial training, and has funded scholarships for young women at Community and Individual Development Association City Campus in South Africa. She appeared on The Oprah Winfrey Show in 2006 and donated one million dollars to Oprah Winfrey's Leadership Academy.

As we have seen from these examples, personal success can enrich the lives of many. You do not have to be a billionaire to make a difference in someone else's life. Philanthropy merely involves improving the life of others and can be accomplished in many different ways. The rewards people feel when engaging in charitable activities is remarkable. Don't think so? Offer to help someone load their groceries into their car. Or the next time you are in line waiting to order coffee, pay the bill for the person in front of you. It may only cost you five dollars, but the positive feeling will last you all day.

Chapter Eight Takeaways

Heraclitus is credited with saying "The only thing constant is change." Although said a couple thousand years ago, it is still true today. Change is constant and everywhere; you must be willing to adapt to new information. If things are not working along your Prosperity Track, find out why and commit to fixing the problem. By routinely tracking your progress, challenges can be identified and rectified. Be proactive and approach experts for advice. If you truly want to become prosperous, be a Prosperity Champion. Share with others what you have learned and achieved. Helping others can be an immensely rewarding experience, further adding to your feeling of prosperity.

Prosperity in Practice

Are you doing what you need to do in order to become successful?

What is working?

What isn't working?

Have you considered enlisting professionals in your journey?

Can your Prosperity Track be an inspiration for others?

Prosperity in Action

Continue completing worksheets regularly.

Identify someone you know who could benefit from what you have learned

Your Next Steps

> *High achievement always takes place in the framework of high*
> *expectation.*
> **Jack Kinder**

Thank you for reading *The Prosperity Track*! I hope that it's been
helpful and has provided you with both inspiration and a roadmap for
your journey along the Prosperity Track. I encourage you to do more
than just read this book. If you haven't already, do the exercises in
this book. They have helped many people just like you get on the
Prosperity Track.

 If there's one theme I hope you take away from *The Prosperity
Track,* it's that your prosperity will depend upon the choices you
make. Over the years, I've had the honor to counsel many people who
are just like you—while they don't have boundless wealth, they
nevertheless seek the freedom only prosperity can bring. They have
achieved prosperity by defining what they really want in life and then

pursuing that vision. Prosperity can be defined in many different ways: a worry-free life, travel, a vacation home, access to higher education, a respected place in the community, and, yes, amassing monetary wealth. The beauty of the Prosperity Track is that it works no matter how you define prosperity for yourself and your family. My job is not to tell you what to value, but to energize, enable, and empower you to reach your goals.

The key is continual effort. I encourage you to turn your good intentions into sustained action. Don't put it off; sit down at the kitchen table and get started today. Determine your guiding values. Make a household budget. Write down your goals. Identify debts that need to be paid off. Chart your progress. If you aspire to live in a mansion, put a photo of a mansion on your refrigerator. If you aspire to travel, put up a photo of your dream destination. Do whatever it takes to keep yourself focused on your goals and not be distracted by passing fads or temptations.

You are capable of being more than you ever dreamed of. As Peter Drucker once said, "If you want something new, you have to stop doing something old." Your success lies just past your comfort zone. It's up to you to go and get the prosperous life you have always dreamed of.

Worksheets

Throughout this book, I have made reference to various worksheets. In this section, I have included images and detailed explanations of these worksheets. You can view and downloaded these worksheets at www.prosperitytrack.com/tools.

The Budget Timeline. This worksheet will help you set a budget at the beginning of each month. Most importantly, it can alert you if your outflows exceed your inflows, possibly causing your checking account to go negative.

Begin completing this worksheet by entering your checking account balance in the box marked "Starting Balance." Then enter your planned expenses, such as rent or mortgage, car payments, utilities, phone, insurance, etc. by the order in which they are due. Make sure you enter the category they belong to (you can add these up at the end of the month to see where you spent the most/least). Next, in the appropriate column, indicate the amount of either income or expense. In the final column, either add (income) or subtract (expense) the amount of the transaction from the previous ending value. Check to see if you have a negative ending balance, since this will require additional funds to pay the upcoming expense.

Budget Worksheet. At the end of each month, add up all the expenses from *The Budget Timeline* worksheet by category and enter them in the *Budget Worksheet.* This will help you track where you earned and spent money throughout the month. This is a great one-page document that you can review in future months and compare income, expenses, and savings.

Debt Management Worksheet. Complete this worksheet at the end of each month to keep track of debts. By keeping an up to date accounting of your debt in one location, you can better assess how your debt management plan is progressing. It is important to keep track of balances, minimum monthly payments, due dates, interest rates, and special circumstances. Proper debt management is essential to achieving prosperity. High levels of debt can severely affect our attitude and even our health. In the "Plan" section, write down debt level changes from the previous month, and your plan for the following month.

Guiding Values. This list contains sixty-four guiding values. Although this list is not comprehensive, it's a great place to start. Begin the exercise by selecting the twenty guiding values you feel best represent you. These twenty values should represent the values you are most *interested* in. Next, cut the list of twenty in half, and select the ten values that are most important to you. You should be *committed* to living these ten values every day. These guiding values should best represent your vision of prosperity. Your happiness and prosperity is contingent upon embodying these guiding values. Dedicate effort and resources to making these values a priority every day.

Personal Balance Sheet. Keeping track of your financial life is important to staying on *The Prosperity Track*. Without viewing trends in both assets and debt, we have an incomplete picture of our financial lives. The goal is not to simply "increase assets" or "decrease debt" but to align your resources with your vision of prosperity. Wealth creates opportunities to be prosperous, but doesn't guarantee it. Rather than focusing solely on assets or debt, I prefer to gauge financial success by assessing net worth. Net worth is the difference between what you have and what you owe. It is the best indicator of whether you are making progress or not.

Priority Spending Calculator. We have limited time and money, yet we have unlimited wants and needs. We must prioritize our efforts and spending to maximize our sense of prosperity. If you have trouble prioritizing your spending, *The Priority Spending Calculator* will help determine your highest and lowest priority expenses.

First, enter your monthly income at the top of the form. You will number the expenses based on their level of priority with one being the highest priority. Begin with your highest priority expense and subtract the amount of the monthly expense from your monthly income and put the total in the column marked "Balance." Next, do this with your second highest priority, and so on. Stay focused, as this can get confusing with many lines in random order (the Microsoft Excel version has a built in feature that will do this automatically). If your balance results in a number below zero, you have an issue with your expenses exceeding your income.

This is not uncommon, as people sometimes have expenses higher than their income. Paying bills will require using money from savings or by borrowing. Without significant savings, this behavior can be detrimental to your prosperity, if prolonged. Look at the list and see if there are areas that can be reduced or eliminated. Evaluate whether the items on your list are indeed needs or wants. If they are wants, consider whether using savings or borrowing money is supportive of your vision of prosperity.

The Prosperity Plan. Once you have completed the exercises in this book, you are ready to create your very own *Prosperity Plan.* Your *Prosperity Plan* will be your roadmap for achieving a prosperous lifestyle. Your plan will include your Vision of Prosperity, Guiding Values, Goals, Strategy Statements, and Milestones & Rewards.

Your *Prosperity Plan* is an evolving document and will need to be reviewed and updated regularly. Circumstances changes and goals get accomplished; it is important your plan remains current and represents your ideal lifestyle. This is your plan; design a strategy to achieve the goals you consider the most constructive to your vision of prosperity.

		Budget Timeline				

Dates _____

Starting Balance [ ]

Date	Description	Category	Income	Expense	End Balance

The Prosperity Track

www.prosperitytrack.com

Budget Worksheet

Dates _____

Income

Employment
Salary, Wages, Tips _____
Business Income _____

Investment
Taxable Interest _____
Non-Taxable Interest _____
Dividends _____
Rental Income _____
Partnership Income _____

Other
Alimony, Child Support _____
Pensions _____
Social Security _____
Other Income _____

Total _____

Expenses

Taxes
Federal Income Taxes _____
State Income Taxes _____
FICA (Social Security)/Self-employment _____

Loan Payments
Mortgage/Rent _____
Auto Loans/Leases _____
Credit Cards _____
Education Loans _____
Other Loans/Debts _____

Insurance
Life _____
Auto _____
Homeowners _____
Long-Term Care/Disability _____
Medical/Dental _____
Liability _____

Household
Food _____
Clothing/Laundry _____
Utilities (electric, heat, water, phone) _____
Household Repairs/Maintenance _____
Auto Expenses (gas/maintenance) _____
Other Transportation _____
Recreation/Travel _____
Entertainment/Dining _____
Charitable Contributions _____
Medical/Dental _____
Child Care _____
Education Expenses _____
Other Expenses _____

Total _____

Net Cash Flow

Total Income [_____]

-

Total Expenses [_____]

=

Net Cash Flow [_____]

The Prosperity Track

www.prosperitytrack.com

Debt Management Worksheet

Date _____

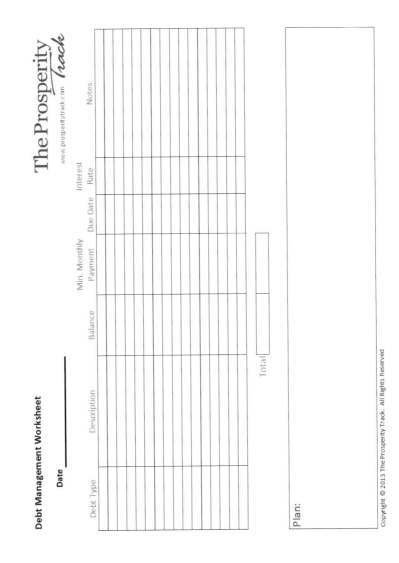

Debt Type	Description	Balance	Min. Monthly Payment	Due Date	Interest Rate	Notes
Total						

The Prosperity *Track*

www.prosperitytrack.com

Plan:

Personal Balance Sheet

Date _____

Assets

Cash/Checking and Savings
Marketable Securities
Non-Marketable Investments
Real Estate/Home
Real Estate/Investment
Automobiles
Personal Property
Personal Loans
Insurance Cash Values
Collectibles
Other
Other
Other

Total Assets

Liabilities

Secured Loans
Unsecured Loans
Credit Cards/Charge Accounts
Personal Debts
Home Mortgage
Investment Debt
Unpaid Income Taxes
Other Unpaid Taxes and Interest
Other Debt
Other Debt
Other Debt

Total Debt

Notes

Notes

Net Cash Flow

Total Assets [   ]

-

Total Debt [   ]

=

Net Worth [   ]

The Prosperity
Track

www.prosperitytrack.com

Guiding Values

Achievement/Success	Generosity	Security
Adventurous	Harmony	Simplicity
Athletic	Health	Spirituality/Faith
Autonomy	Honesty/Integrity	Spontaneous
Beauty	Hope	Strength
Big-Picture	Humility	Supportive
Challenge	Humor	Sustainability
Committed	Inclusive	Teamwork
Community	Independence	Trust
Competition	Initiative	Variety
Consistent	Innovation	Wealth
Courage	Inspiring	Wisdom
Creativity	Intelligence	
Curiosity	Love/Affection	
Discipline	Loyalty	
Diversity	Motivated	
Duty	Nurturing	
Education	Optimistic	
Effectiveness	Passionate	
Efficient	Patience	
Empathy	Positive	
Excellence	Power	
Family	Productivity	
Flexibility	Recognition	
Friendship	Reliable	
Fun-loving	Respect	

Priority Spending Calculator

Date _____

Income _____

Need/Want	Amount	Priority	Balance
Federal Income Taxes			
FICA (Social Security)/Self-employment			
State Income Taxes			
Food			
Prescriptions/Medication			
Mortgage/Rent			
Homeowners Insurance			
Utilities (electric, heat, water, phone)			
Household Repairs/Maintenance			
Child Care			
Auto Loans/Leases			
Auto Insurance			
Other Transportation			
Auto Expenses (gas/maintenance)			
Medical/Dental Insurance			
Life Insurance			
Clothing/Laundry			
Credit Cards			
Education Loans			
Other Loans/Debts			
Long-Term Care/Disability Insurance			
Recreation/Travel			
Entertainment/Dining			
Charitable Contributions			
Education Expenses			
Savings			

The Prosperity Track

www.prosperitytrack.com

The Prosperity
Plan

Date: _____

Vision of Prosperity

Guiding Values

1.	2.	3.	4.	5.
6.	7.	8.	9.	10.

Goals

Internal	External	Relationship
1.	1.	1.
2.	2.	2.
3.	3.	3.
4.	4.	4.
5.	5.	5.

Strategy Statements

I will
I will
I will
I will
I will
I will
I will

Milestones & Rewards

Milestone	Reward
1.	1.
2.	2.
3.	3.
4.	4.
5.	5.

The Prosperity
Track

www.prosperitytrack.com

Made in the USA
San Bernardino, CA
18 September 2013